DIFFERENCE

In the 1970s, the concept of 'difference' transformed our understanding of language and our reading of literary texts. Since then it
has found application in almost every branch of literary and cultural
studies. In this accessible, lively volume, Mark Currie traces the
diverse meanings and changing fortunes of the term from a wide
range of sources in philosophy, linguistics, feminism, cultural geography and cultural theory.

The author follows the concept from its most widely studied articu-
lations in structuralism and poststructuralism to broader critical
issues such as individuality, diversity and universality. He offers
particular discussion of:

- Identity and difference
- Difference and reference
- Differance
- Different histories
- Cultural difference
- Difference and equivalence

D1388568

Displaying a remarkable range of discussion and unique insight
into underlying philosophical and social debates, *Difference* is the
best possible introduction to a term at the very heart of recent critical
thought.

Mark Currie is Professor of English at Anglia Polytechnic University
in Cambridge. His previous publications include *Metafiction* (1995)
and *Postmodern Narrative Theory* (1998).

THE NEW CRITICAL IDIOM

SERIES EDITOR: JOHN DRAKAKIS, UNIVERSITY OF STIRLING

The New Critical Idiom is an invaluable series of introductory guides to today's critical terminology. Each book:

- provides a handy, explanatory guide to the use (and abuse) of the term
- offers an original and distinctive overview by a leading literary and cultural critic
- relates the term to the larger field of cultural representation.

With a strong emphasis on clarity, lively debate and the widest possible breadth of examples, *The New Critical Idiom* is an indispensable approach to key topics in literary studies.

Also available in this series:

DIFFERENCE

Mark Currie

Routledge
Taylor & Francis Group

LONDON AND NEW YORK

First published 2004
by Routledge
2 Park Square, Milton Park, Abingdon, Oxon OX14 4RN

Simultaneously published in the USA and Canada
by Routledge
270 Madison Ave, New York NY 10016

Reprinted in 2004

Routledge is an imprint of the Taylor & Francis Group

Typeset in Adobe Garamond and Scala Sans
by Keystroke, Jacaranda Lodge, Wolverhampton
Printed and bound in Great Britain
by TJ International Ltd, Padstow, Cornwall

British Library Cataloguing in Publication Data
A catalogue record for this book is available from the British Library

Library of Congress Cataloging in Publication Data
Currie, Mark, 1962–
    Difference / Mark Currie.
        p. cm. — (New critical idiom)
    Includes bibliographical references and index.
    1. Philology. 2. Difference (Philosophy) I. Title. II. Series.
    P121.C87 2004
    400—dc22
                                    2003020295

ISBN 0-415-22221-4 (Hbk)
ISBN 0-415-22222-2 (Pbk)

Contents

SERIES EDITOR'S PREFACE

The New Critical Idiom is a series of introductory books which seeks to extend the lexicon of literary terms, in order to address the radical changes which have taken place in the study of literature during the last decades of the twentieth century. The aim is to provide clear, well-illustrated accounts of the full range of terminology currently in use, and to evolve histories of its changing usage.

The current state of the discipline of literary studies is one where there is considerable debate concerning basic questions of terminology. This involves, among other things, the boundaries which distinguish the literary from the non-literary; the position of literature within the larger sphere of culture; the relationship between literatures of different cultures; and questions concerning the relation of literary to other cultural forms within the context of interdisciplinary structures.

It is clear that the field of literary criticism and theory is a dynamic and heterogeneous one. The present need is for individual volumes on terms which combine clarity of exposition with an adventurousness of perspective and a breadth of application. Each volume will contain as part of its apparatus some indication of the direction in which the definition of particular terms is likely to move, as well as expanding the disciplinary boundaries within which some of these terms have been traditionally contained. This will involve some re-situation of terms within the larger field of cultural representation, and will introduce examples from the area of film and the modern media in addition to examples from a variety of literary texts.

Acknowledgements

I am very grateful to John Drakakis, Mary Dortch and Monica Kendall for their excellent editorial suggestions in the writing of this book, and to Liz Thompson, Fiona Cairns and Linda Paulus for their patient assistance. Whether they know it or not, there are many others who have influenced its content, and particular thanks are due to Simone Tongue, Sarah Maguire, Rebecca Stott, Nigel Wheale, Rachel Potter, Drew Milne and Graham Allen. I am very grateful to Alex Warwick, who turned this into a far better book than it would have been. I would like to thank Antony Gormley for the little people on the cover, who say it all. And I dedicate the book to my brother Nick and my sister Emma.

1

INTRODUCTION: IDENTITY AND DIFFERENCE

The concept of difference is unusual among critical terms. While others come and go, difference has persisted. While others are confined to some particular critical perspective or approach, difference has found applications in almost every branch of literary studies, and perhaps more significantly, beyond the domain of literary studies. One explanation for this unusual scope might be that the term encompasses some very familiar, easily available meanings. What could be more straightforward than the idea of difference? It is the opposite of sameness.

Perhaps the two most convenient and commonplace ways of explaining the meaning of a word are to relate it to other words meaning the same thing (synonyms), as dictionaries do, and to relate it to words meaning the opposite of it (antonyms), as I have just done. Often these two kinds of explanation will amount to the same thing. The dictionary definition of 'difference' offers 'unlikeness', which is a synonym by virtue of the fact that it negates its antonym.

By relating the word 'difference' to its opposite, the dictionary and I have gone some way to explaining its meaning, but we have also introduced the way that the word 'difference' might act as a principle for explaining how words get their meanings in general. I have explained 'difference' through the concept of difference, in that I pointed to the difference between it and another word. Or I defined it negatively, in relation to its opposite, as if the meaning of its opposite were given in nature and could act as a foundation for any other word that related to it. In fact if I tried to explain the meaning of 'sameness', I would find it very difficult to do it without reference to the concept of difference, so that its solidity as a foundation is compromised and my definition becomes rather circular. My definition of difference has nowhere to rest, and I find myself rebounding between one word and the other indefinitely.

This suggests that the meaning of words inheres in their relations with each other, that words have no foundations, and meanings are not self-contained. This idea, that the meaning of words is produced by their relationships with each other, or their differences, and that there are no foundations, is often referred to as a 'relational' account of meaning.

The relational view of meaning is clearer if the words 'sameness' and 'difference' are left out of it for the moment, since in the discussion so far, they are both the objects and the method of the analysis. If I had started from the words 'night' and 'day', this would not have arisen, because the problem that I am describing in the designation of meaning would not have contaminated the very words that I am using for the description. In another sense, the words night and day might have been easier because they are less abstract. It could be argued that night and day *are* given in nature. Their meanings seem less dependent on each other, and more bound up with their ability to refer to something outside of language. What we have here is a dichotomy and a complication. The dichotomy is between a relational and a referential view of linguistic meaning. The complication is that we can't get outside of language to describe how it works, because we still have to use words to describe the way that words work.

The philosophical, cultural and political scope of this set of arguments may not be apparent immediately, but comes into focus when the word sameness is substituted by the word 'identity'. As synonyms, 'sameness' and 'identity' are both antonyms of 'difference'. This translation helps to explain the broad and interdisciplinary career of the term 'difference' which, in literary studies at least, began life as an obscure and technical term in structural linguistics. The opposition of identity and difference is slightly more complex because identity is synonymous with both sameness and difference: the dictionary defines identity as both 'absolute sameness' and 'individuality' or 'personality'. The slippage here derives from an ambiguity about the points of comparison and antithesis that are in operation. 'Identity' can clearly mean the property of absolute sameness between separate entities, but it can also mean the unique characteristics determining the personality and difference of a single entity. In itself this points to a view that is also reached through a labyrinth of linguistic and cultural theory: that the identity of things, people, places, groups, nations and cultures is constituted by the logics of both sameness and difference.

There are two ways of making sense of this co-dependence. The first is to point out that the sameness of one identity group is often constructed through a sense of difference from another, so that some common denominator is posited among Scots through the sense of opposition with the English, or among women through difference from men. The second is that even if (or perhaps because) identity relies on some external difference, there is also internal difference. This is obviously true of the largest unities such as nations: that we might momentarily posit some common denominator among Greeks, but at another level the unity is comprised of individuals who all differ from each other. But it is also true at the level of the individual. If I think of my own identity, I do not encounter a straightforward, indivisible singularity, but a plethora of places, times, roles, functions, interests, opinions and physical characteristics. I am a 'multifarious polity of denizens', as Robert Louis Stevenson describes the multiplicitous nature of a human being in *Dr Jekyll and Mr Hyde*, to the point where the words 'me' and 'I' seem to be under considerable strain. If I am unique, it is not because I am singular and indivisible. If anything it would be the opposite, that I am differentiated internally and in relation to others in many different ways. Personal identity, like words, appears to have an undeniable relational component, and as with the relational account of language, the relational account of personal identity comes with the complication that one cannot really stand outside it in order to consider what it is.

These sorts of arguments indicate the imbrication, or the inseparability, of words with issues of identity and difference. It is arguable that every noun is marked by this kind of dialectic of identity and difference, and that every political or philosophical debate to some extent turns on the ways that this dialectic operates. A noun effectively does two things every time it is used. It asserts a difference at the same time as it denies a universe of differences. If I say 'dog', I assert a difference because I posit a common denominator between dogs that distinguishes them from cats but I also do a terrible injustice to the rich diversity of dogs, effacing the irreducible individuality of each member of the set. In this sense every noun is a category, or a generalisation, a potential collective identity and a potential stereotype. Most nouns involve this double process of saming and differentiating, of positing a common essence between members of the set and at the same time marking the differences that give the set its identity.

The stakes of this double process are clearly not confined to philosophy. If the double logic of saming and differentiating is inherent in most nouns, it clearly has to be at work everywhere, every time we name an entity or an identity. The importance of this can be stated in two steps. The first is to point out that naming has the immense power of being a process that we take completely for granted. We use nouns automatically, repeatedly, habitually, without reflecting on the differences they establish and repeat. Nouns become an index of entities that we take for granted, in the sense that we reassert their existence, their common denominators and their points of difference. The more automatically, habitually and unproblematically nouns are used the more entrenched becomes the framework of differences they impose on the world.

The second step, then, is to ask the question of what it is that we are automatically subscribing to when we use nouns and names, and what can be done about it. One way of understanding the importance of the critical concept of difference is to see it as a way of reflecting on the tenacity of certain problems in the world. And the basis of this tenacity is simply that the words we use to name the things in the world are often mistakenly assumed to be passive reflectors providing an index of the entities that exist in the world, or a list of differences discernible between things. It could be argued, for example, that the difference between men and women is taken completely for granted as an aspect of the world because it is so deeply embedded in the language system. Paul de Man (1919–83) describes this mistake as a confusion of linguistic and natural reality, and uses it as the basis of a definition of ideology. This book will explore this definition at several points in later chapters: that is, the view that to accept words automatically, to take them for granted, or to consider differences to be properties of nature is to subscribe to something that might loosely be called *ideology*. Ideological critique often finds its starting point in the opposite view, namely that words project a system of differences on to the world: that differences are not properties of the objective world being described as much as they are properties of the language describing the world. Using language, then, is not a passive process of describing the world but an active process of construction, or *structuration*, even when we believe otherwise. Language makes us think of constructed things as if they were natural, and this is why linguistic differences are ideological, but if so, ideology simply becomes another condition to add to the list of conditions that we cannot get outside of.

FROM PHILOSOPHY TO LINGUISTICS

The concept of difference, then, is a central part of one of the funda-mental problems in philosophy, and its full genealogy really lies in the emergence of the problem of identity in philosophy over several centuries. And yet this is not the impression that one would receive if one's read-ing were confined to the realm of Anglo-American literary criticism and theory, especially that between 1965 and 1985. This was a period in which much of the intellectual energy in criticism and theory was being drawn from the discovery of structuralist models of analysis, models that were formulated mostly in France, but that were widely and insistently represented to an Anglo-American critical community in the 1970s and 1980s. The impression given by these mediations of structuralism is that the term 'difference' originates in the work of Ferdinand de Saussure, a Swiss Professor of Linguistics at the University of Geneva whose lectures were collected together and published posthumously as *Course in General Linguistics*. It is not my intention here to deny the importance of Saussure's linguistics, nor the fact that he gave to the concept of difference a particu-lar philosophical valence (which I will describe shortly), but there is something very strange, and worth analysing, about the order of events through which 'difference' became established in the Anglo-American critical lexicon. Saussure's course of lectures was delivered between 1906 and 1911, not published in French until 1915, and not translated into English until 1959. Even then, it took some time for Saussure's name to find its way into critical and theoretical discussion in the Anglo-American world. From about 1970 it happened like an avalanche, with Saussure's linguistics and the structuralist methods it inspired being mediated to the English-speaking world through works such as Fredric Jameson's *The Prison House of Language* (1972), Jonathan Culler's *Structuralist Poetics* (1975) and Robert Scholes's *Structuralism in Literature* (1974), a host of translations of the work of Roland Barthes, Jean Piaget, Emile Benveniste, Gérard Genette and Tzvetan Todorov, and then a second wave of guides to the structuralist analysis of just about everything. In Britain, for example, Methuen's (now Routledge's) New Accents series published a long list of titles whose role in the dissemination of structuralist analysis now seems inestimable, including at least six volumes published before 1985 that root the concept of difference in Saussurean linguistics: Hawkes's *Structuralism and Semiotics* (1977), Fiske and Hartley's *Reading Television* (1978), Hebdige's *Subculture: the Meaning of Style* (1979), Belsey's *Critical Practice* (1980), Elam's *The Semiotics of Theatre and Drama* (1983) and Waugh's *Metafiction* (1984). One of the most striking things about the New Accents series is the repeated exposition of structural linguistics from volume to volume as a way of establishing the linguistic basis for the concept of difference.

There are some important and closely related observations to be made from this publishing history about the emergence of the critical concept of difference. The first is that the world of Anglo-American literary studies was given every reason to see difference as a Saussurean, and as a structuralist invention, and very little reason to view the Saussurean conception of difference as a facet of an ongoing philosophical problem. In Britain it is quite understandable that Saussurean linguistics was viewed in isolation from philosophical problems about identity and difference if only because the philosophical provenance of difference is much easier to establish in relation to Continental philosophers, such as Kant, Hegel, Kierkegaard, Nietzsche, Husserl and Heidegger, than in home-grown philosophy. But it is not just that the context of Continental philosophy was relatively absent in the reception of structuralism in Britain. It could be argued that the philosophical context as a whole was rather neglected in the process of establishing difference as a critical term.

The next important observation is that, after this de-contextualisation of difference as a self-contained structuralist invention, there came a rather confusing episode for the New Accents generation of critics, namely the arrival of *poststructuralism*. Again, there are profound oddities here, not least that in France there was no equivalent word until much later, and that the United States had experienced little more than a brief encounter with structuralism before what we now call poststructuralism arrived on its shores. But the more important confusion here lies in the fact that for those who viewed difference as a structuralist issue, there was some surprise that so-called poststructuralist works in translation, like Jacques Derrida's *Writing and Difference* (1978) and later Gilles Deleuze's *Difference and Repetition* (1994), seemed only very remotely related to structural linguistics. Derrida's work, where the concept of difference undergoes some of its most important transformations, in fact makes very little reference to Saussure. There is a much-cited section in *Of Grammatology* about the relationship between speech and writing in Saussure's *Course*, an extended discussion in the essay 'Differance', and beyond that really only short references and allusions to the Saussurean account of difference. Similarly, in Deleuze's major work, *Difference and Repetition*, there is one brief reference to Saussure, and only occasional gestures elsewhere, usually with the intent of distancing himself from the field of linguistics in general. Several commentators on Deleuze, such as Jean-Jacques Lecercle and Brian Massumi, have been at pains to point out that Deleuze's approach to language is more closely derived from the Stoic philosophers than from Saussure. My point here is that difference is often misrepresented either as an entirely structuralist issue, or more specifically, as a Saussurean invention. But to represent difference in this way is to ignore the much broader context, and longer history, from which it derives its unusually complex meanings and uses. There is extended discussion of Derrida's relationship with Saussure in chapters 2 and 3 below, but it is worth saying at the outset that Derrida's approach to Saussure is to view his concept of difference as merely one example of an entire heritage of western metaphysics, a concept rather uncritically inherited from philosophy along with a lot of unrecognised presuppositions and assumptions. The kind of originary importance that the New Accents series sometimes ascribed to Saussure is in fact a prime target for what came to be known as deconstruction, and this will be discussed at some length in chapter 2 in relation to Derrida's neologism *differance*.

I say all this as a kind of caution against a rather limited historical scheme which sees difference as a structuralist invention subsequently modified by poststructuralist interventions. Anyone who subscribes to this view will struggle to make sense of many poststructuralist writings on difference, where the coordinates are mainly pre-Saussurean. In other words, if it once seemed that poststructuralism had grown out of structuralism, or that the poststructuralist approach to philosophy rested on linguistic premises – propositions about the nature of language and the basis of linguistic meaning – it now looks as if the supposed origins of difference in Saussure's *Course* were in fact not origins at all, and that what is often supposed to have come later (poststructuralism) is in fact a demonstration of what produced the supposed origin in the first place. The persistent reader will discover that this is one of Derrida's favourite games, that is, the critique, perhaps *deconstruction*, of origins according to a logic of *supplementarity*. The logic of supplementarity, which lies at the heart of deconstruction, can be crudely summarised for the moment as follows: that sometimes things that come afterwards can be seen as conceptually prior to the origins from which they supposedly follow.

There is a tendency in poststructuralist writing, exemplifed in supplementarity, towards counter-intuitive logical complexity of this kind, sometimes accompanied by opaque levels of abstraction and an overuse of terminology that occasionally descends into hollow verbiage. The emphasis placed on Saussure in the New Accents series was one way of ensuring that it did not descend into this opaque theoretical language. The fact is that Saussure's *Course* is one of the clearest statements anywhere of a relational account of identity, and not only that, but of the problem that I described earlier as the imbrication of language in questions of identity. It is not then that Saussure's concept of difference is the source of all relational identity thinking, but that it is a wonderfully clear account of what relational identity means. There are two broad characteristics of twentieth-century philosophy that Saussure encapsulates, the first being the view that philosophy undergoes a shift from an attention to things in themselves to an attention to the relationship between things, and the second being the view that philosophical problems in the twentieth century are invariably problems about language. A succinct expression of both of these philosophical tendencies can be found in Saussure's proposition, that 'in language there are only differences, and no positive terms' (1983: 118), which seems to suggest not only that the relations between words are all-important, but also, if there are no positive terms, that these differences might actually constitute the positive content of that word. I will be taking a close look at the implications of this sentence in the next chapter. For now, I would like to observe that it is without doubt the most cited proposition in Saussure's work. It is this proposition that is usually laid down as the foundation stone for those accounts of difference that use Saussure as an origin. A reading of Saussure often produces a surprised reaction to the quite technical use he makes of the word 'difference', his preference for the word 'value' as an account of the way in which meaning is generated by difference. One of Saussure's basic moves is to view the linguistic sign (that is, the word), as a two-sided entity, but where the two sides are inseparable, or joined together in the brain by an associative bond. These two sides of the sign are the *signifier* and the *signified*, which Saussure defines as the sound and the concept respectively. This is a more interesting and controversial claim than it sounds, because if the signifier and the signified are inseparable (Saussure describes them as analogous to the two sides of a piece of paper (1983: 111)), and the value of a sign is generated by differences between words, as Saussure claims, it follows that the signified content of a sign is not a thing in the world but a linguistic relation. Or to put it another way, this is an account of the sign that does not start in reality, does not anchor the sign as a nominalistic view of language would do, in the world of things. It is exactly this point that many of his structuralist disciples found appealing in Saussure's account: that there is no extralinguistic reality to guarantee the meaning of words.

It is possible to see already the importance of this account of the sign for a relational theory of identity, but this importance becomes more transparent when another of Saussure's key observations is added in. The relationship between the signifier and the signified, he claims, is *arbitrary*. Again this claim seems uncomplicated at first sight, and can be taken to mean that there is no reason to attach a particular signifier to a particular signified. There are a few rare cases in which a reason might reasonably be advanced, such as the onomatopoeic sign, in which the signifier actually sounds like the signified, and is therefore 'motivated' rather than arbitrary (such as 'splash'). But in most cases the only thing that bonds the signifier to the signified is linguistic convention, which repeatedly glues a particular signifier to a particular signified through the pure force of repeating the association. We might just as well use the signifier 'bear' to signify a spherical object and the signifier 'ball' to signify a furry quadruped, but convention decrees it the other way around. But the arbitrary nature of the sign might be said to involve more than this. Many structuralists also saw in Saussure's *Course* the more profound suggestion that if signifiers were joined to signifieds in signs, and the value of signs was generated by differences between words rather than pre-existing differences in the world, there was also something arbitrary about the way that a language system divided the world up. There was a revealing cultural relativist point to be made here about the way that different languages could divide the world up differently, and thereby produce in their linguistic subjects, by which I mean the speakers of those languages, entirely different ways of seeing the world. There is a little academic sub-industry, not to mention a species of the chattering classes, that roots itself intellectually in the observation that the Inuit language has many more words for snow than the English language. But however much repeated this observation is, it does represent a philosophical view that the discriminations between entities that we think of as the natural world are enabled by the vocabulary to name these differences.

LINGUISTIC DIFFERENCE AND CULTURAL DIFFERENCE

Though Saussure refers to a large number of different languages in the *Course* and devotes a whole section towards the end to the geographical diversity of languages, the cultural relativist interested in language and difference will find a more discriminating account in the work of American linguists Edward Sapir (1884–1939) and Benjamin Whorf (1897–1941) than Saussure's *Course*. Sapir's work in particular presents a culturally deterministic view that linguistic difference and cultural difference might actually be the same thing:

> The fact of the matter is that the 'real world' is to a large extent built up on the language habits of the group. No two languages are ever sufficiently similar to be considered as representing the same social reality. The worlds in which different societies live are distinct worlds, not merely the same world with different labels attached.
>
> (1949: 162)

Difference, in Sapir's account, is a culturally relative way of making discriminations, and the system of differences in a language system therefore becomes the reality of that culture. I referred earlier to the automatic and habitualised way in which people use language, and Sapir has an equivalent view, that in speaking one's own language, one is often 'anaesthetised' to it, and therefore prone to a sleepy assumption that its system of discriminations is a straightforward reflection of an objective, rather than a social, reality. It was this kind of account of the ideological function of language, of the relation between linguistic and natural differences, that many people located in Saussure's view of language as a system of differences. Of course there are arguments still to be had, not only about whether Saussure intended this meaning of arbitrariness as the cultural contingency of a linguistic system of differences, but also about whether this is arbitrariness at all. It could just as easily be argued that the example of the many Inuit words for snow is not some arbitrary cultural difference but an important difference of linguistic motivation between those surrounded by snow and those who know it more distantly. It could easily be said that Inuit culture has a set of interpretative requirements that demand finer discriminations, and therefore that these different requirements motivate the linguistic differences that we find encoded in different languages. Similarly, we could say that within a culture we find a considerable degree of internal variation in vocabulary determined by particular interpretative requirements. The skier with some basic avalanche training, for example, might be closer to the Inuit reality than to that of the Venezuelan lifeguard, in the same way that the Customer Services personnel at a paint manufacturer might have the linguistic power to distinguish a multitude of colour shades that the general population might be unable to see, let alone name. In other words, Saussure's concept of difference has some suggestive cultural resonances which are opened up by the basic relativism and relationality of his thesis about signs.

But if we are looking for the legacy of Saussure in the analysis of cultural difference there is another story to tell. It is a striking feature of Saussure's teaching that he loves to illustrate the nature of language by analogy. To illustrate the importance of the system of differences in assigning value to a sign, Saussure will often invoke an analogous question of identity. One well-known example of this is the analogy of the train, which features in the discussion of what he calls 'synchronic identities' in chapter 3 of the *Course*. Saussure points out that trains, like signs, are systems of differences without positive terms in the sense that the identity of the 8.45 from Geneva to Paris is not substantial but relational. This is to say that the coaches and engines that make up the 8.45 from Geneva might never actually be the same units, but as long as the differential relations between the 8.45 and, say, the 7.45 from Geneva are maintained, the identity of the train is secured. The 8.45 is in fact perceived as the same train regardless of which day of the week it departs:

> We assign identity, for instance, to two trains ('the 8.45 from Geneva to Paris'), one of which leaves twenty-four hours after the other. We treat it as the 'same train', even though probably the locomotive, the carriages, the staff etc. are not the same . . . the train is identified by its departure time, its route, and any other features which distinguish it from other trains.

> (1983: 107)

He makes the same point of the chess board: that it is not necessary for the pieces on a chess board to conform to any particular formal conventions so long as the system of differences between pieces is preserved. In other words, a bishop does not need a mitre for the game to work as long as it remains distinguishable from other pieces. Once again, there is nothing substantial about a chess piece which gives it its identity. Rather that identity derives from the overall system in which pieces are differentiated in relation to one another (Saussure 1983: 108–9). It is easy enough to press these analogies further into questions of identity. Do the substantial components of a human being constitute that person's identity? Is it not true that many cells and particles of a human body are cyclically reproduced in much the same way as the rolling stock of a train is altered? The consequence of this kind of analogy might be to say that human identity inheres much more obviously in the system of social relations than it does in the body. But whether this is true or not, that people are merely differences without positive terms, the point I want to highlight is that there is something in Saussure's account of the linguistic sign that actually militates against difference. The real individuality, the concrete particularity, the unique substance of the train or the chess piece are effaced here by the concept of difference. It could in fact be said that the concept of difference is no respecter of difference in so far as it sees identity entirely in relational terms.

It can also be argued that identity in general, perhaps the identity of a person, or that of a social group, are also subject to these principles. A theory of subjectivity, or personhood, for example, might locate identity not in the body of the individual but in the relations between that person and others. In other words a person might not be defined by inherent characteristics, but like Saussure's train or chess piece, be understood as an identity only because of the relationships that person has with other people, in a system of family, friendship and social relations. This would be referred to as a relational view of personal identity. The same might be said of collective identities. It might be argued, for example, that a national identity is not one that is made up of inherent qualities (of 'positive terms' in Saussure's language) but of relational ones concerned with how a nation distinguishes itself from other nations. Some have used these ideas of relational identity to point to the importance of a system of differences in any group identity. Jonathan Culler, for example, has argued very persuasively that 'travellers' define themselves as a group only in relation to, or more exactly in opposition to, 'tourists', and that the sense of difference from tourists is a much more important factor in the identity of a traveller than any inherent characteristics that the group might possess (Culler 1988: 153–67). All these relational theories of identity effectively deny difference in the same way as do Saussure's examples of the train and the chess piece. For this reason there is something quite paradoxical about the term 'difference' because it can on one hand designate individuality and particularity, and on the other, designate the principle of relational identity that denies that particularity. What we are encountering here is another version of the paradox, encountered at the start of this discussion, that identity contains two apparently opposite meanings, namely sameness and difference.

It is quite common to find the concept of difference described in critical and theoretical commentary as a kind of celebration of diversity, of individuality and particularity, and yet it is clear that the opposite is also true: that 'difference', is a critical concept that looks for the systematic (or systemic) basis for meaning, and the relational context for identity. There is what I would see as a kind of abuse of the term difference which invokes it in defence of freedom and individuality, and a system of values associated with liberal pluralism and tolerance. And yet, in the reception history of the concept, there is also a consistent opposition to the term and the kind of analysis it implies on the basis that the structuralist concept of difference actually abstracts the entities it analyses to the extent that they are emptied of all particularity and individuality. This is a charge that was levelled against literary structuralism throughout the period of its influence in the twentieth century: that the rich diversity of literary texts were reduced by structuralism to an arid set of differences, of relationships, and to an abstract level at which some systemic common denominator could be perceived. This accusation will be considered more fully in chapter 1.

Similarly, the concept of difference as it is adapted to anthropological analysis finds itself charged with an eradication of difference for the same reason: that it does not consider things in themselves, but rather the relations between things. Claude Lévi-Strauss, an anthropologist born in 1908, is one who adapts the Saussurean model of language to the analysis of social relations in such a way that the analysis yields structural homologies across cultural difference. If we wish to celebrate the individuality and particularity of things in the social world, we might say, for example, that no two families are the same, on the grounds that they are comprised of unique individuals in unique combinations. But if we look at Lévi-Strauss's work on the subject of the family, we find him talking of the family as the *unit of kinship*, in which a *set of relations* between family members forms *a global system*, a *structure of correlative oppositions* held in place by the *universal presence of incest taboo*. Everyone's favourite uncle, in Lévi-Strauss, is abstracted into the *avunculate*, which is a characteristic trait of an elementary structure of more complex systems of sociality. So incongruous is the relation between structuralist analysis and the object of study sometimes that it can be hard not to see it as an absurdist parody of social science, and yet it was exactly this kind of scientific gravity that the Saussurean model imported into literary studies in the mid-twentieth century. And this is not an emphasis that is always understood in relation to the term difference: that whatever it was to become later, the term 'difference' started its life in literary criticism in the most austere of scientific contexts, less as a celebration of difference than as the agent of a preposterous equivalence between things.

Against the background of this global scientific project, the post-structuralist intervention in the career of the term 'difference' is easy to characterise. There was a feeling, in the work of many thinkers after 1965, that the homogenising forces of the structural linguistic model should be resisted. Difference had become a machine for containing difference, for reducing it to similarity or packaging it neatly in the closure of the binary opposition. In chapter 3 below, I will be analysing the critique of the structuralist model of difference in relation to Derrida's neologism *différance*. For now, I would merely point to the most basic characteristics of this critique, one of which is identifiable in the phrase *irreducible difference*. If structuralist analysis tended to look for an abstract level of equivalence between disparate phenomena (the sameness of all folk tales, the structural similarities between different weddings, the equivalence of the myths of Jesus and Dionysus, etc.) the poststructuralist will often insist on the irreducibility of differences to such abstract equivalences (each story is unique, each wedding is particular). At one level, this insistence operates as I have already described it, as an opening up of assumed unities, such as words, into the multiplicities that they contain. But the idea of irreducible difference can also be seen as a fundamental change in the way that philosophers and critics understand the relation between language and the theory or metalanguage that describes it.

This argument can be made as follows. The assumption of much structuralist analysis is that structure is an objective property of the object being analysed, namely the system of differences making meaning possible. But for many poststructuralists, this emphasis on objective structural properties is a mistake, so that structural homologies between one text and another, or one family and another are not to be understood as somehow given in nature. They are, rather, similarities and equivalences actually produced by the model of analysis, in the sense that the structuralist simply asks the same questions about disparate objects, and in so doing, actually generates the same answers. If, for example, you ask a question about the chemistry of a tree, you get a chemical answer, and similarly, if you ask a structural question about a literary text, you produce a structural answer: the object is not simply given in nature, but represents the result of an analytical interpretation that is determined by the nature of the question addressed by the analysis. In other words, the structuralist is not so much discovering some previously hidden similarity between things. The structuralist is inventing that similarity, generating it with the model of analysis, or actively *saming* things that are in themselves neither similar nor different.

This relationship between the method of analysis and the thing analysed is sometimes known as the deductive model of theory, whereby the model itself comes first and subsequently projects its own structures and assumptions on to the thing it claims to be analysing objectively. According to this model, the analysis produces the object. One of the characteristic strategies of a poststructuralist analysis is that it will do the opposite, that is, take an individual literary text and use it to destroy the model of analysis through a demonstration that the text itself will always exceed, or fail to be contained by, the analytical model seeking to reduce it. Or, to put it another way, the irreducible difference of a text can always be used to resist the homogenising forces of systematic analysis, which seek to establish homology across difference. In such a demonstration, the idea of irreducible difference works according to an inductive relationship between theory and text in the sense that theoretical knowledge is extracted from an individual text, and not projected on to it by the method of analysis.

Poststructuralism derives quite a lot of its energy from exactly this kind of disruption of, and resistance to, the scientific pretensions of structuralism. A much favoured poststructuralist ploy, for example, is to mock the structuralist view of the binary opposition as the basic unit of difference. If difference, after all, is confined to opposition we are dealing only with what Deleuze calls the maximum of difference, and neglecting the many minor calibrations and nuances of the middle ground. Deleuze is one of many poststructuralists whose work can be seen as a kind of opposition to opposition, or an attempt to liberate thinking from the strictures of opposition and open it to multiplicity. The opposition and its closest relatives (the contradiction, the dialectic) are abstract forms of difference which represent a limited way of understanding the true scope of multiplicity and diversity. This opening up of opposition in poststructuralist thought has to be taken alongside a second characteristic strategy, which is to expose the opposition as a power relation, in which one term dominates the other, and the deconstructive strategy in relation to such oppositions, which entails the reversal of that hierarchy. These approaches to, and modifications of, the concept of difference are examined in detail in the following chapters.

It is no doubt apparent that this vocabulary of difference, even when it emerges from a formal linguistic system, is laden with social and political significance. It is undoubtedly this social resonance that has ensured the persistence of difference as a critical term beyond its philosophical and linguistic provenance. So far, we have touched on several areas in which the linguistic concept of difference could be said to furnish some kind of social theory.

(1) The structuralist view of the sign aims to articulate an apparently free-standing term into the system of differences that is the basis of its intelligibility, and the basic meaning-generating unit is the binary opposition. For the structuralist there is always an unconscious relation to an opposite that gives a sign its meaning. It is, I think, fairly easy to perceive the social logic implicit in this account: that a social identity is structured by an unconscious relation to an opposite. Like a word, a social identity has a hidden structural condition in the form of a relation to an other. This basic structuralist insight is now widespread as a foundation for feminist and postcolonial accounts of gender and cultural difference.

(2) In structuralist theory, the opposition tends to be described as an innocent dyad, or an antonymic relation, without heed to questions of power or hierarchy. Poststructuralist approaches to opposition tend to introduce the notion that one term enjoys some privileged or assumed superiority over the other, and it is a common deconstructive strategy to overturn such a hierarchy. This importation of power into the opposition gives difference a decidedly political inflection, or a structural logic for the description of established hierarchies and their revolutions.

(3) The opposition comes to be seen after structuralism as a reductive or oversimplified paradigm for difference, and it is particularly in the domain of social and political critique that this reduction is evident. It may be that there is still a place for the opposition in political thought, but postmodern cultural theory has shown a preference for a liberation of difference from the confines of opposition, and for the multiplication of difference into ever more complex configurations. Complex social totalities such as genders, nations or indeed the world have, in a sense, followed linguistic theory into more multifarious and complex theories than the opposition.

(4) The structuralist account of the sign bears very close affinities with other philosophies of relation. One such affinity can be seen in the

Freudian tradition of psychoanalysis in which the notion of the 'other' has come to occupy a prominent place. Psychoanalytic theory has been a source of particular power for the description of social identity and has been adapted for sociological purposes by feminist, postcolonial and even Marxist critics, who have found in it a fundamentally structuralist theory of identity and identification. The relation of psychoanalysis to poststructuralism will be the subject of further discussion, but for the moment it may be worth contemplating a single issue related to the topic of opposition. Freud's phrase 'the narcissism of minor differences' is a particularly resonant one for the analysis of social logic. It refers to the narcissistic process by which individuals or groups tend to compare themselves to people only very slightly different from themselves, and subsequently construe that nuance of difference in oppositional terms. Scottish identity, for example, seems more closely predicated on a relation with the English than it does on a relation with those, say the North Koreans, whose cultural difference might seem more major. Sometimes, therefore, the other is not really an opposite at all, and yet in structural terms, it remains the hidden structural condition in which an identity finds its basis.

(5) It has been clear in this discussion that the logic of difference and the logic of equivalence are themselves structurally connected, to the point at which one seems to transform into the other. This has been shown to be true of the structuralist concept of difference, but might apply equally to the logic of globalisation. For example, it is clear that as the world contracts towards the condition of a village under economic pressures towards standardisation, that differences by no means disappear. This co-dependence of standardisation and diversification will figure at length in the discussion of globalisation and difference in chapter 5.

It is not that the social theory of difference simply learnt everything it knows from linguistics. But it is clear that the concept of difference has a rather unusual power to link the realms of social identity, philosophy, political power and the nature of language. It is the aim of this book to describe the logical and associative links that give the concept of difference this power, and therefore to offer an account of its durability. The chapters that follow explore the concept of difference as it develops from a quite specific linguistic term into a key idea in cultural criticism. Chapter

2 is concerned with the role of difference in the analysis of a sentence, and the way that the analysis of a sentence acts as a model for the analysis of much longer discourses, such as literary narratives. It is particularly concerned with the way that difference reshapes the way that literary critics think about the relationship between fiction and reality by questioning fundamental assumptions about the relationship between the form and content of a narrative representation. Chapter 3 summarises some complex critiques of structuralist approaches to difference which are developed in the work of Jacques Derrida and Gilles Deleuze, two French philosophers whose work has had a considerable influence on the Anglo-American literary critical tradition. The chapter aims to describe a kind of rebellion against binary oppositions, which takes place after structuralism, and which leads towards a less rigid, static and scientific concept of difference. Chapter 4 explores the ways in which concepts of difference guided developments in new historicist criticism from the 1970s to the 1990s, and particularly the way that history has been rewritten, literary canons revised, literary texts reinterpreted and revalued to accommodate cultural differences. Chapter 5 is concerned with concepts associated with difference, such as 'alterity' and 'otherness' as they have influenced feminist and other politically orientated critical approaches. It describes a sociological context for difference in a 'globalising' world in which cultural differences become more visible against the threat of 'standardisation' and looks at the way that various philosophers and cultural theorists have linked cultural differences with the contemporary condition of the world known as 'postmodernity'. Finally, chapter 6 raises some questions about what has been lost as a result of the prominence of difference as a critical and cultural perspective. It argues that the concept of difference has given recent literary criticism a particularist character, in the sense that it is more concerned with particular details than theories and categories, and points to some sources of theory that might allow for the return of a kind of universalism in criticism. It is therefore a consideration of the possibility that, after the recent history described throughout the book, the career of difference as a critical concept might be coming to some kind of an end.

2

DIFFERENCE AND REFERENCE

What exactly did Saussure mean when he said that 'in language there are only differences, and no positive terms' (1983: 118)? One view is that words do not really have positive content: the meaning of words is not only generated by, but actually constituted by their relationships with each other, and not by their relationship with an outside world. This might seem an extreme or over-hasty interpretation, but it does represent a widely held view of the significance of difference: that it places in question the whole idea that language can refer to reality. A more considered conclusion might be that language does not simply and unproblematically refer to reality, that reference is not the only way to think about language, nor is it really separable from questions about the formal systems of language. It is the aim of this chapter to show that difference can be thought of as a general term for the various types of relations between words involved in the production of meaning, but also that these types of relations can apply equally to literary texts. This chapter is therefore a description of the way that ideas about difference not only place in question the idea that individual words might refer, but also the idea that sequences of words, such as sentences, or novels, or texts in general, might equally be seen as elaborate systems of differences and relations and therefore not simply as representations of reality.

PARADIGMATIC AND SYNTAGMATIC RELATIONS

A useful starting point here is that there are two major categories into which differences, or relations between words, can be divided. The first category is relations *in praesentia*, or relations between any word and the other words with which it combines in a sequence. The second category is relations *in absentia*, or relations between words that are present and those that are absent from a given utterance. Linguistic meaning is obviously deeply bound up with both of these categories of relations. To generate a meaningful sentence, for example, one has to be able to do two things simultaneously: to combine words with each other in a chain, and to select the right words from all the available possibilities for each position in the sentence. The factors that govern these two principles, of combination and selection, are extremely complex. The meaningful combination of words in a sequence, for example, will involve a kind of grammatical competence, or knowledge of the rules and practices that govern the order in which elements of a sequence are arranged; but other factors will be in play, such as the logical linearity of the sequence, or the need for emphasis or elegance to maximise the effect of the sequence. Similarly, the principle of selection entails an extremely complex, assimilated knowledge of the language system as a whole, an ability not only to select the right kind of word for each position, but to understand its relations of similarity and difference, synonymity and antonymity, with the other available possibilities. Of course, this all happens automatically, and need not be calculated each time from first principles, but it is partly the automatic and uncalculated ability to do something so complex that is the interest for linguists, philosophers and critics. When we tie a shoelace, we hardly notice the astounding complexity of the knot or the incredible dexterity required to tie it, and that pales in comparison to the creation of a complex sentence. In both cases, the fascination of the process is only accessible when it is de-automated, or defamiliarised, so that its nature can be grasped anew. At its best, this is what the structuralist analysis of these types of relations achieves.

The categories of combination and selection are in effect ways of defamiliarising the automatic and unobserved processes involved in the production of meaning. In 'Two aspects of language and two types of aphasic disturbances', Roman Jakobson (1896–1982), a Russian-American linguist, looked at cases in which a linguistic disorder makes visible the processes of meaning production that we would normally take for granted, namely the ability to select and combine words. Jakobson is interested in the fact that aphasia takes one of two forms – that it is a disorder in the ability either to select or to combine words in intelligible ways – and from this he extrapolates that the production of meaning takes place on two axes: the axis of selection and the axis of combination. These two axes, which are essentially the ones described by Saussure in the *Course*, formed the basis of a widely deployed system for the analysis of linguistic relations. For Jakobson and many who followed him, the two categories of relations between words were named as *syntagmatic* relations, which pertained to the axis of combination, and *paradigmatic* relations, which pertained to the axis of selection. I will return to the importance of this system for the concept of difference shortly. For the moment it is worth pointing out that this highly ordered approach to the study of linguistic relations was not plucked out of the air by structuralists in the mid-twentieth century. It was in fact a well-established principle, known particularly well to the classical rhetoricians. The importance of this lies not only in the recognition that there is something classical in the structuralist approach to language. It also helps to define the importance of difference to literature.

The study of rhetoric was primarily a science governing the production of eloquent and effective language. The founding idea of rhetoric was that the kinds of skills to be found in the discourses of the naturally eloquent speaker could be systematised and learned by those less naturally gifted. In a sense this is akin to the structuralist system which analyses and renders visible what is normally intuitive, except that rhetoric was orientated towards the production of eloquence rather than a general science of language. It was the commodification of a natural gift, but in the process it was also a kind of Aladdin's cave of linguistic descriptions and principles. Classical rhetoricians divided the art into five stages – *inventio, dispositio, elocutio, memoria* and *actio* – which can be crudely translated as thinking up a topic, arranging it, adding effects, memorising it, and acting it out. It is the middle stage of this classical system, *elocutio*, that bears the closest resemblance to structuralist accounts of meaning. *Elocutio* was the stage in which patterns and figures were integrated into the presentation in such a way that the discourse would have maximum persuasive impact.

These effects were in turn divided into two major families, which had several different names in the history of rhetoric, but which came to be known most commonly as *schemes* and *tropes*. Effects that depended on the ways in which words and sentences were combined together in sequence were named schemes, while effects deriving from the principle of selection were named tropes; or to return to Jakobson's terminology, there are language effects deriving from syntagamatic relations, and effects deriving from paradigmatic relations.

There are always going to be some difficulties with this kind of hard and fast categorisation, and the story goes that fierce arguments used to rage in the Roman forum about whether antitheses such as *paradox* and *oxymoron* were schemes or tropes. The rhetorical prehistory is relevant to the structuralist account of linguistic relations in two ways: first, it undermines the idea that structuralism was some radical new departure in its approach to linguistic performance; and second, it places the axes of selection and combination in a more direct relationship with literary language, since the prehistory of rhetorical schemes and tropes effectively provides structuralist poetics with a way of describing specifically literary effects.

This ought not to be overstated. There was always a sense in which the structuralist concept of difference was indifferent to the cultural value of its object: it was not analysing beautiful or persuasive language, but aiming to describe the universal principles of language. Jakobson described poetics (the study of literature) as a subset of the global science of linguistics, and defined the poetic function of language as 'the projection of the axis of selection into the axis of combination'. This is a perplexing definition, but is probably reducible to something like this: literary language differs from ordinary language in the degree to which it mixes effects derived from the principle of selection with those derived from the principle of combination. In structuralist poetics there is always a sense of incongruity between the dry systems of linguistic description and the assumed value of literature. Much of the controversy surrounding structuralist dealings with literature is generated from this incongruity. But in fact structuralism was merely developing a time-served approach to literature, and if anything giving it a broader application. It could be argued that literary structuralism was no more an unwanted intrusion of science into the realm of literature than the extension of rhetorical analysis outwards to language in general. The reciprocity here between literary analysis and linguistic science is really just the result of the generality of the principles underlying the analytical categories. One view would be that these are simply the categories of time and space, categories as fundamental to dry science as they are to rhetoric or the description of aesthetic beauty, so that the terms we have been considering might be arranged thus:

Time	Space
Combination	Selection
Syntagmatic	Paradigmatic
In praesentia	*In absentia*
Schemes	Tropes

It is certainly clear that these are categories that can be applied to the analysis of anything. If I take my life, for example, I can freeze it in time at any moment and analyse it as if spatially, as a kind of existential moment in which I could have chosen, paradigmatically as it were, to do otherwise. The nature of each moment can then be understood in terms of the things I decided not to do, the places I didn't go, the things I didn't say, and from that point of view the meaning of the moment is constituted by the absent possibilities from which I chose. Alternatively I can analyse a moment in terms of its place in a chain, in a sequence, so that the moment acquires its significance in relation to prior and subsequent moments, by its syntagmatic relations with them. These principles can clearly apply to anything, and are surely only separable for analytical purposes. They are observable in the dichotomy between synchronic and diachronic history, the former freezing time while the latter narrates across time. Sometimes one is privileged over the other, as in Jean-Paul Sartre's existential psychoanalysis, where lives are diagnosed in relation to moments of crucial, life-determining choice without much respect for the complex sequence of events, of continuities and repetitions, which place people in particular situations and limit their freedom to choose at given moments.

In the case of literary structuralism it is hard to know which principle was more important. On the one hand the major impact of the concept of difference derived from its paradigmatic meaning, of relations between words in the language system, or relations *in absentia*, and the suggestion that these relations were the basis of meaning. And yet on the other hand, when it came to a literary text, there was a limit to the value of pointing to absent words or episodes as the basis of intelligibility, and attention was directed instead at the internal structural relations in a discourse. An account of the importance of Saussurean linguistics, for example, will almost always emphasise the profound recognition that the relationship between a signifier and a signified is arbitrary, and therefore that there is also something arbitrary about the way that differences between words determine the entities contained in the universe. The emphasis in this kind of account is on the paradigmatic meaning of difference, since it refers to the relation between a given word and those other words in the language system that delimit its meaning. But any detailed application of structuralist linguistics will usually leave this principle behind and focus on the internal relations between components of a discourse. Structuralist narratology, for example, is characteristically concerned with the syntagmatic pole of difference, and focuses on questions such as the meaning-generating function of opposition in a narrative sequence, or the temporal order and structure of narrative.

Shortly, I will return to look at the way a structuralist analysis of narrative deploys these perspectives on difference. First I want to look at the analysis of a simple sentence in terms of its syntagmatic and paradigmatic relations. If I take the sentence 'The man ran down the road' I can easily point to the principles of combination and selection at work in its construction, using a diagram.

		Selection
	Dog	
The man ran		**down the road**
	Cat	
	Woman	
	Darkness	
	etc.	

Combination

The syntagmatic relations between the words in the simple sentence in the diagram are those that can be read horizontally along the axis of combination, and so are the relations between co-present words. The paradigmatic relations are those that can be read vertically, and if written out in full, would represent the entire set of words in the language system that could be placed in that particular position in the sentence, absent words that could be substituted for those present. Obviously the paradigms for the words 'the' and 'down' are small in number, whereas for the other words the range of possible substitutes is enormous. For obvious reasons then, the task of describing the syntagmatic relations in this sentence is relatively simple, whereas the task of describing paradigmatic relations for the word 'man' is vast and has to be reduced to something more manageable. One way of doing this is to limit the set of substitutable paradigms to what might be called *significant others*, or words in relation to which the present word most directly derives its identity. This is where the binary opposition becomes important for structural linguistics: that the meaning of the word 'man' is above all determined by its oppositional relation to the word 'woman'. This is an obvious point, but there is a subtlety here that needs to be explored. In pointing to the binary opposite as the significant other, the structuralist is not really saying that the writer of the sentence has consciously chosen the word 'man' over the word 'woman'. There is a sense in which the category of choice, and therefore the principle of selection, is a bit misleading here. What is important about the binary opposite for the structuralist, is precisely that it is a hidden, assimilated and unconscious structural relation, and it is exactly because a writer or speaker does not choose consciously to exclude the opposite term that the structuralist reconnects it with the hidden structural system on which its meaning depends. We might think of words as free-standing, but for the structuralist they cannot be properly understood unless they are articulated back into the system of differences that underlie and enable their apparently free-standing significance. I said earlier that the classical science of rhetoric was also a means of systematising something that was intuitive, unconscious and natural. The subtlety that I want to explore here, however, is that there is a kind of slippage between the intentional and the unconscious, between the production and the analysis of language, or between value judgement and neutral science.

This slippage is most apparent when the rhetorical system of schemes and tropes is compared to the structuralist system of syntagmatic and paradigmatic relations, or when the implicit value judgements of rhetorical analysis find their way into the apparently value-free science of structuralism. Rhetorical analysis characteristically subdivides the families of schemes and tropes into various categories. Schemes, for example, are often subdivided into categories such as *phonological schemes, morphological schemes* and *phrase and clause schemes,* which can be defined as patterns of combination concerned with sound, word structure and sentence structure respectively. Tropes, on the other hand are usually divided into two distinct types of selection or substitution, namely *metaphor* and *metonymy,* where a metaphor is based on the principle of comparison, and metonymy on the principle of contiguity. Most of these can be illustrated in relation to the sentence in the diagram above. There are sound schemes for example in the repetition of vowel sounds (man/ran) or initial sounds in words (ran/road) known as *assonance* and *alliteration* respectively. The creation of a trope, on the other hand would depend on the substitution of other words such as 'darkness', or perhaps 'size 10 boots', for the word 'man', generating in the first case a metaphor based on a perceived similarity between the action of a man and the movement of darkness, and in the second, a form of metonymy known as *synecdoche,* in which a part of something is substituted for its whole.

For the rhetorician, patterns and substitutions of this kind lie at the heart of creative and effective language use. They are, in effect, verbal skills on which the persuasive impact of language is based. From the point of view of rhetorical analysis then, the identification of schemes and tropes always carries with it an implicit value judgement, as a typology of creative or persuasive moments in a discourse. This kind of typology obviously has particular relevance to the analysis of literature, or at least of literariness, since it is in effect a species of evaluative stylistics: a kind of analysis that identifies categories in which the enormous variety of creative, inspirational and brilliant acts of combination and selection can be grouped. But this evaluative dimension to the identification of schemes and tropes begins to look rather distant from the structuralist enterprise. The structuralist is self-fashioned as a scientist indifferent to the aesthetic value of language. The structuralist, I have already claimed, is concerned to defamiliarise the unconscious and automated complexities of language.

But what I have been describing here seems to be more focused on acts of conscious artifice, on creative choice and on artful patterning. I think it can be suggested that with rhetorical analysis as a prehistory, it was always difficult for literary structuralism to rid its analytical descriptions of this evaluative dimension, or to move completely away from the assumption that paradigmatic and syntagmatic relations in language were part of the conscious and intentional level of artistic production.

TRANSPARENT AND OPAQUE LANGUAGE

The questions of value judgement, and of conscious intention, in literary structuralism are particularly complicated ones, and will resurface at various times in the discussion that follows. For the moment it will be worth reflecting on how these issues about syntagmatic and paradigmatic relations bear on questions about the referentiality of language. Again here it is useful to think about the ways in which structuralist conceptions of difference extended perceptions about language that were well known to rhetoricians into more radical philosophical claims. To begin with, traditional rhetorical analysis had always been familiar with the idea that language might at times be primarily about itself. Rhetorical and formalist analysis will often talk of *marked* or *foregrounded* language to describe language that is somehow visible in its own right. Schemes and tropes are, in a sense, linguistic phenomena of stylistic interest that stand out from the humdrum, the familiar and the automatic. Because poetry is commonly viewed as a genre of discourse in which the incidence of schemes and tropes is at its most dense, it is also commonly viewed as a kind of writing in which *what is said* is subordinate to *the way in which it is said.* Prose, on the other hand is thought of as a kind of writing in which the content of the discourse is not so much obscured by, or subordinated to, the way in which it is expressed. This is what is meant by the distinction between opaque and transparent language. Opaque language is that which draws attention to language itself, to style, to verbal form and to the way that something is said, whereas transparent language effaces itself, allows itself to be looked through, and points towards content. In the case of opaque language, such as poetic diction, we are likely to ask questions about images and patterns, whereas in the case of transparent language, such as prose fiction, we are more likely to ask questions about content, or the world depicted. Of course these distinctions are crude. It is easy to think of poles of transparency and opacity *within* poetry and fiction (*Pride and Prejudice* and *Finnegan's Wake* perhaps), or to regard the distinction as merely different kinds of style, or different orders of content. But the terms are useful for the description of the impact of difference on questions of reference.

The use of terms such as 'foregrounded' or 'marked' implies that some language stands out, and that it can be distinguished from other kinds of relatively invisible language use. One of the things that distinguishes the structural analysis of language is that, as a science of language in general, it shows particular interest in the apparently transparent, invisible language that traditional literary analysis neglects. In other words it aims to show that all language works in the same way, and therefore to question the traditional view that some kinds of language are more transparent than other kinds. This is where the radical reputation of structural linguistics and literary structuralism comes from: the proposition that the transparency of everyday or prosaic language is just an illusion; or that the language of prose fiction is just as opaque, just as orientated towards form, as the language of poetry. A word like 'dog', for example is commonly thought of as a transparent signifier in the sense that we look through the word and see the animal, or the concept of the animal, the signified. But for the structuralist, there is something invisible going on, which has to be made visible for language to be properly understood. It would be difficult to say what mental pictures are conjured in the mind by the word 'dog', but easy enough to say that the picture would have to exclude objects that are patently not dogs, such as cats. The structuralist is therefore saying that the referential function of the signifier 'dog' is an illusion which depends on the existence of other signifiers from which it differs. These other signifiers are not obviously present, and yet it is their presence in the language system on which the meaning, the concept, or the picture associated with the word 'dog' depends. In this sense, the words that are not there, the paradigms of the words 'dog', invisibly inhabit the word that is there, and are the structural conditions required for 'dog' to refer. This dependence that any word has on the system of differences in which it operates makes it much less easy to view a signifier as a transparent medium. Rather than look through it to the thing that it names in the world, what we are doing is believing ourselves to be looking through it when in fact we are looking at it, since it is constituted by the trace of other signifiers that form its system of differences. This is revolutionary, because suddenly dogs do not exist as natural objects visible through their names, but become concepts by virtue of the system of differences between signifiers. What the structuralist is saying, then, is this: that if we continue to believe that dogs are a natural category named by the signifier 'dog', we will fail to notice that a system of differences between signifiers is projecting its structure on to our concepts. We must not look through words. We must look at them, and sideways, to the absent others that are the basis of any signifier's intelligibility.

This raises a complication, which is probably one of the biggest areas of controversy in structuralist theory. It means that opacity is not so much a property of a linguistic sign per se as a way of looking at it or analysing it. It is as if we must resist the commonsensical view of language as a transparent and referential medium, resist the presence of worldly objects in language and look instead at the way that the language system manufactures those objects through difference. It is as if this is a superior way of seeing adopted by those initiated into the arguments of structuralism, while the rest of the world continue to be duped by the illusion of linguistic transparency. And this is exactly the impact of structuralism in universities: the displacement of an everyday intuition with a highly counter-intuitive way of looking at language as capable of referring only to itself, to its own form and system. It is an unnatural, or denaturalised way of looking, which is required in order to make visible the constructedness of things normally assumed to be natural or given. In the second half of this book, this kind of argument is explored in its political context, where the entities under discussion are more controversial than dogs, and the imperative to look at, rather than through, language, becomes a political one.

POETICS, SEMIOLOGY AND NARRATOLOGY

This then is the recurring emphasis of structuralism: to render visible the unconscious structures of language, and to defamiliarise the automatic processes of linguistic selection and combination. The term 'difference' in literary and social theory therefore carries within it a whole set of arguments about the opacity of language, the illusion of reference and the constructedness of reality. But how does this actually work when it comes to the analysis of a literary text? As with the word, it is characteristic of structuralist literary analysis to view a literary text counter-intuitively, as a system of signs which do not, as we might assume, simply point to or even simply imitate the real world. This is particularly obvious in relation to fiction, where the view of literature as a mimetic medium is the most difficult to displace. Yet critics such as Gérard Genette and Tzvetan Todorov succeed in treating fictions as opaque, non-referential discourses by scaling up grammatical categories and the principles of syntagmatic and paradigmatic relations to describe the system of a novel exactly as if it were a sentence. Hence, for Todorov, relations *in praesentia* and *in absentia* are the basic categories for discussing the components of a narrative sequence, and he develops a lexicon of linguistic terms for the description of these relations. In the work of Jakobson and Roland Barthes, the scientific and linguistic character of fictional analysis operates alongside an explicity theoretical polemic against the traditional idea of realism in the novel. It is probably these arguments about realism that have given literary structuralism its radical reputation, and for many they seemed to extend the absurdly exaggerated view of the linguistic sign developed in structural linguistics as a non-referential entity. The exaggeration is that the linguistic conditions that make reference possible – the systems of differences, conventions and codes – are elevated to the status of referents, so that meaning is not only enabled but actually constituted by difference. Fredric Jameson, for example, argues in *The Prison House of Language* that structuralist criticism came to view the form and system of narrative as its only content:

> The most characteristic feature of structuralist criticism lies precisely in a kind of transformation of form into content, in which the form of structuralist research (stories are organised like sentences, like linguistic enunciations) turns into a proposition about content: literary works are about language, take the process of speech itself as their essential subject matter.
>
> (1972: 198–9)

It was common, before structuralism, to think of the content of a narrative fiction as a world of characters and events. The content of *Pride and Prejudice*, for example, is an assemblage of people in interaction, a complex set of circumstances in which the Bennet daughters seek husbands, and most centrally, Elizabeth moves towards her union with Mr Darcy. But if, as Jameson suggests, the 'essential subject matter' of the literary work is language and form, this kind of realistic subject matter, made up of characters and events, is displaced. The displacement can be viewed in two ways. The first view is that form and language are simply more important kinds of content than characters and events, so that the structuralist critic simply sweeps the latter aside, brackets it, in order to focus on more pressing aspects of the text. The second is that characters and events are in fact comprised of language and form, that Elizabeth Bennet is no more than a concatenation of verbal signs organised in a narrative form, and that to think of her as a person with a life is to mis-understand the true nature of textual content. Both of these views of the relationship of form and content are found in structuralist criticism, but it is fair to say that it is the second that underlies the most influential acts of structuralist criticism. Saussure says in the *Course* that the signifier (the sound) and the signified (the concept) are like two sides of a single sheet of paper, that one cannot cut through one without also cutting through the other. This is the view that is characteristically offered by structuralists of the relation between language and its referential content in a narrative fiction: that one cannot cut through the form and language of a novel without also cutting through its characters and events.

If we stick with the question of fictional character for a moment, the transition in criticism from realistic inferences to descriptions of semio-logical systems of differences is easily charted. Perhaps the seminal work in this context is by Vladimir Propp, a Russian formalist critic whose treatment of narrative is, in effect, proto-structuralist, though not trans-lated into English until the mid-twentieth century. Particularly important in this regard is Propp's *Morphology of the Folktale* (1928) in which he argues that fairy tales are, structurally speaking, basically the same as each other. Propp makes this case in a number of ways, but the central move is to argue that characters in the narratives fulfil a limited number of *functions*. In this move, there is a clear departure from the assumption that a character is a representation of a person, to the view that the character is a function in a grammatical system, and can be best understood as a kind of device in the construction of a plot. Hence, for Propp, there were certain boxes into which characters could be cast – villain, donor, helper, princess, dispatcher, hero and false hero – which abstracted the individuality of that character into a grammatical function. In 1966, A. J. Greimas developed Propp's insights into the plot-functions of characters in *Semantique Structurale*. This is a work providing one of the most robust statements of the period of the importance of difference, opposition and negation as fundamental structures of thought and language. Greimas describes differences, for the most part, as existents in the world we perceive, and that we subsequently register in our languages, but there is also a sense in which differences become the mechanism for making the world take shape, as an arrangement of differences that he calls *semes*, or units of meaning that differ and form binary oppositions.

Like Propp, Greimas sees a fictional character as a linguistic function and not a person, and he names this function an *actant*. The system he develops for the analysis of a story, the *actantial model*, is based on the view that the oppositional structure of a plot is created by the arrangement of actants in a certain sequence according to a limited set of possibilities. Greimas's basic aim with the actantial model is to show not only that all stories, when abstracted in this way, enact the same deep structure, but that stories are merely an instance of structural rules common to all sentences. A fictional plot is, for Greimas, generated from three sets of oppositional differences: subject and object, sender and receiver, and helper and opponent. The category of subject and object, for example, allows for the analysis of desire narratives, such as *Pride and Prejudice*, to be emptied of their specific content, and become a set of relations between actantial roles, narrative paradigms and syntagms, chosen and arranged in a manner analogous to the principles of sentence production described above. According to the actantial model, then, there is to be no speculation on the subject of whether Mr Darcy loves Elizabeth. At best there might be some disagreement as to whether Elizabeth is the subject or the object of the actantial structure.

The actantial model is one example of the way that literary strucuralism seeks general rules and structural homologies (or logical similarities) between narratives, and might therefore be accused of destroying difference – that is using the principle of difference to find abstract similarities between narratives that are, in their particularity, different from each other. It also represents clearly the way that oppositional semes can be both paradigmatic and syntagmatic features of a narrative. We might, for example, view the opposition of a hero and a villain as the basic dyad from which narrative meaning is generated, but we might also see it, or other oppositions in a plot, in temporal terms. Structuralists will often view the beginning of a plot and its ending in the terms of an oppositional structure, so that a narrative can be seen to enact a passage from one pole to another, from happy to sad, young to old, single to married, or alive to dead. This translation of temporal opposition into spatial opposition is at best a confirmation of the Jakobsonian formula, that literature projects the axis of selection into the axis of combination, but is also an example of the kind of move objected to by poststructuralist critics, namely the synchronization of diachronic aspects of language.

It is worth observing that Greimas's system for the analysis of character is another example of a rather ambiguous mode of *defamiliarisation*. If realism is a mode that aims to make the devices of fiction invisible, Propp and Greimas are critics intent on the baring of those devices. But Propp, like his fellow Russian formalists, worked with a fairly straight-forward distinction between realism, which sought to make the devices of language imperceptible, and anti-realism, which sought to call attention to those devices. It is more difficult with Greimas to determine whether the acts of defamiliarisation, of alienation from language, of baring the devices, or exposing the hidden conditions of meaning, belong to the work under analysis or the critical act itself. As I have said, it was the major impact of structuralist criticism to claim that transparent and opaque language were operating in the same conditions, and therefore to give the impression that the hidden conditions of linguistic structure could be conflated with the content of a discourse. With the actantial model of narrative, as with the structural account of the sign, it can be difficult to determine whether the system of differences enables, constitutes or prevents linguistic reference. The actantial model, then, is a good example of what Jameson means when he talks about the transformation of form into content. It takes the traditional idea of character, conventionally under-stood as fictional content, and translates it into a system of differences to be understood as formal arrangement in the text.

It is worth reflecting now on what kind of critical approach to narrative is emerging from the concept of difference. First, we have a belief that the model of syntagmatic and paradigmatic relations for the analysis of a sentence might be extended into a theory for the understanding of a longer discourse. Second, we have a perceived similarity between these structuralist categories and the precepts of classical rhetoric. Third, there is a tendency, as exemplified by Greimas, to view the organisation of narratives primarily in terms of opposition, and particularly abstract opposition, in the sense that the particular content of a narrative, such as a character, is emptied of that particularity for the production of structural homologies between different narratives. Taken together, these three tendencies provide a context for Roland Barthes's influential manifesto, 'Introduction to the structural analysis of narratives'. Beginning from structural linguistics, Barthes is concerned to outline a 'second linguistics' capable of dealing with units of meaning larger than the sentence, but this project will have to be distinct from classical rhetoric for the following reason:

> Discourse has its units, its rules, its 'grammar': beyond the sentence, and though consisting solely of sentences, it must naturally form the object of a second linguistics. For a long time indeed, such a linguistics of discourse bore a glorious name, that of Rhetoric. As a result of a complex historical movement, however, in which Rhetoric went over to belles-lettres and the latter was divorced from the study of language, it has recently become necessary to take up the problem afresh. The new linguistics of discourse has still to be developed, but at least it is being postulated, and by the linguists themselves. This last fact is not without significance, for, although constituting an autonomous object, discourse must be studied from the basis of linguistics. If a working hypothesis is needed for an analysis whose task is immense and whose materials infinite, then the most reasonable thing is to posit a homological relation between sentence and discourse insofar as it is likely that a similar formal organization orders all semiotic systems, whatever their substances and dimensions.
>
> (Barthes 1977: 83)

Here we have a kind of abstract of the argument so far in this chapter: that linguistics offers a basis for the analysis of longer discourses, that a narrative is homologous with a sentence, and that rhetorical analysis became derailed along the way as a result of its own preoocuaption with beauty and elegance. It is also worth noting here that Barthes is referring to Emile Benveniste when he claims that linguists themselves are postulating this new, second linguistics. But this is not an uncontroversial issue, as a reading of Geoffrey Strickland on the subject will reveal (Strickland 1981: 127–44). In fact it was never clear that something as complex as a novel could be analysed on the same basis as a sentence, and Barthes clearly floundered in his own attempts. The model of paradigmatic and syntagmatic relations is relatively easily deployed in the analysis of a sentence, partly because the units of meaning being selected and combined are easily identifiable. Saussure, for example, talks mainly about selection and combination at three levels of meaning: the phoneme, the morpheme, and the word. But what do we do when dealing with an entire narrative discourse? What units of meaning are there beyond the level of a word that might allow the narratologist to deploy the model for the analysis of narrative in general?

These are questions that have been answered in different ways by different narratologists. Todorov, for example, offers quite a simple account of the units of a narrative discourse by reducing a story to a set of abstract propositions. In a manner similar to Propp, a folk tale can be expressed as a set of abstract propositions in the following way:

X is a young girl
Y is a king
Y is X's father
Z is a dragon
Z abducts X

(Todorov 1981: 49)

Having identified these minimal units in narrative, Todorov goes on to describe various aspects of the narrative proposition. He begins with the distinction between agents and predicates. Agents are more or less the same as actants, in the sense that they are roles to be filled by beings, usually human, and are represented here by X, Y and Z. In these abstract propositions, therefore, names such as Mary and John can be substituted for X and Y, and something dragon-like for Z. Predicates, on the other hand are the story's verbs (to be a young girl, to be a dragon, to abduct, etc.). In this simple scheme there is already a complex set of paradigmatic and syntagmatic relations. Most obviously, the roles represented by X and Y can be occupied by a large number of possible beings, so that X and Y might be occupied by Mary and John, but equally by Hermione and Theobald. The characteristics attached to characters in a fictional narrative are also selected, so that X and Y could vary in moral character, appearance, or anything else. Perhaps less obviously, each narrative proposition is itself a paradigm, in the sense that an entire proposition can be substituted for another. In this schema, for example, 'Z abducts X' might be changed for any number of alternatives, such as 'Z abducts Y' or 'Z kills X'.

Equally, the analysis can identify syntagmatic aspects of the narrative schema, concerned not with the selection of agents, predicates and propositions, but with the way in which they are combined in a sequence. Here again, the question of how minimal units combine in a sequence is a gateway into an enormous narratological topic. Todorov describes the sequence as 'a higher unit', meaning that it is not a narrative proposition, but a logic that links the narrative propositions together, and that can work in a number of ways. For a more complex account of the numerous narrative possibilities governing the sequence, Todorov points to the work of Boris Tomashevski and Claude Bremond, both of whom have attempted to draw up schematic charts of the many possibilities of combination of narrative units. To give a flavour of the possibilities of combination, he describes the sequence of the ideal narrative as follows:

> An ideal narrative begins with a stable situation that some force will perturb. From which results a state of disequilibrium; by the action of a force directed in a converse direction, the equilibrium is re-established; the second equilibrium is quite similar to the first, but the two are not identical.

(1981: 51)

This is one kind of abstract and structural analysis of which literary criticism has been aware for a long time: that a narrative sequence can be reduced to a basic scheme which begins with stability and order which is then disrupted before a similar state of order is restored. Its value to this discussion is that it suggests two categories into which narrative units might fall, namely units describing a state and those performing a transition from one state to another. Thus, a unit such as 'Y is X's father' describes a state, whereas 'Z abducts X' transforms the stable state of their family relations into one of crisis and disorder. Roland Barthes names these categories as *indices* and *functions*, and points out that many indices in a narrative can be omitted for the purposes of describing the sequence of a narrative, however important they may be to the narrative as a whole. It is clear that, when describing the syntagmatic or sequential aspects of a narrative schema, it is the second type of unit that is most essential to the description of the sequence because it is the predicate of change. If, for example, I wanted to describe the sequence of *Pride and Prejudice* in a hurry, I would emphasise the narrative units that Barthes calls 'functions', which have a role in the transformation of one state to another, such as Darcy's rudeness at the Netherfield ball, Wickham's elopement with Lydia, or Elizabeth's trip to Derbyshire with the Gardiners.

If we now return to the question of the type of critical practice that emerges from the structuralist concept of difference, it is clear at least that it produces a highly abstracted and formal kind of analysis. The structuralist essentially empties a narrative of most of its details in order to identify the deep structural principles operating beneath them, and so uncover the system of relations that organises those details. We might view this as a kind of criticism addressing itself less to the question 'What does a narrative mean?' than to the question 'How does it mean?' Or to change the wording slightly, this looks like a kind of criticism orientated towards the form rather than the content of narrative. But is this really the case? And how do we get from this mere critical orientation to Jameson's claim that structuralism actually transforms content into the essential subject matter of a work? Suppose we take another example of this kind of formal analysis at work, a case that I will borrrow from Terry Eagleton's highly influential *Literary Theory: an Introduction* published in 1983. To illustrate the transformation of form into content in structuralist analysis, Eagleton outlines a very simple story:

> Suppose we are analysing a story in which a boy leaves home after quarrelling with his father, sets out on a walk through the forest in the heat of the day and falls down a deep pit. The father comes out in search of his son, peers down the pit, but is unable to see him because of the darkness. At that moment the sun has risen to a point directly

overhead, illuminates the pit's depths with its rays and allows the father to rescue his child. After a joyous reconciliation, they return home together.

(1983: 95)

Like Todorov, Barthes and others, Eagleton's concern here is to schematize the story into units of narrative, which he does as follows:

The first unit of signification, 'boy quarrels with father', might be rewritten as 'low rebels against high'. The boy's walk through the forest is a movement along the horizontal axis, in contrast to the vertical axis 'low/high', and could be indexed as 'middle'. The fall into the pit, a place below ground, signifies 'low' again, and the zenith of the sun 'high'. By shining into the pit, the sun has in a sense stooped 'low', thus inverting the narrative's first signifying unit, where 'low' struck against 'high'. The reconciliation between father and son restores an equilibrium between 'low' and 'high', and the walk back home together, signifying 'middle', marks the achievement of a suitably intermediate state.

(1983: 95)

A tone of spoofery runs through this illustration of the structuralist method, but as an illustration it draws attention to some interesting problems in the relationship between form and content. The first observation that Eagleton makes about this method is that 'it brackets off the actual content of the story and concentrates entirely on the form'. This observation is supported by the claim that one could replace the key agents (father and son, pit and sun) with entirely different elements (mother and daughter, bird and mole) and still have the same story: 'As long as the structure of relations between the units is preserved, it does not matter which items you select' (1983: 95). A question arises immediately here which places in question the first claim that this method concentrates entirely on form: surely the structural relation of 'high' and 'low' depends on the referential content of the words 'sun' and 'pit'? We could go on to say that to construe the relation of father to son as part of the same high/low opposition depends not only on the referential content of 'father' and 'son' (the father being bigger than the son) but also on the symbolic content of the relationship of father to son in terms of authority. What Eagleton seems to mean by form, therefore, is simply a schema based on content, but at a higher level of abstraction. The sophisticated structuralist defense to this objection would be that the words 'pit' and 'sun' only have referential, or indeed symbolic, content because of their systemic relations in the language system: their complex relations with synonyms and antonyms delimit and act as the conditions for the production of their referential content: in short that their content is constituted by their formal relations to other words in the language system. But if this argument is accepted, it simply means that it is inaccurate to say that structuralist method brackets off content and concentrates exclusively on form. It would be more accurate to say that the method conflates content and form to the extent that they cannot be separated, and a formal schema in this kind of narratology is merely a content-based abstraction.

Of course this issue is not passed over by Eagleton, who remarks that 'there is a sense in which the sun is high and pits are low anyway, and to that extent what is chosen as "content" does matter' (1983: 96). So one of the things that the reading illustrates is the characteristically contradictory position of structuralist criticism on the question of referential content. First he says that content is ignored, then that it actually determines the formal schema it was supposed to have displaced. This apparent contradiction is probably nothing more than the collision of two analytical frameworks: an old one in which form and content are categorically separate and a more modern one in which one cannot cut through the form of language, or narrative, without also cutting through its content, as if form and content were the two sides of a sheet of paper. It is on the basis of this second analytical framework that Jameson can claim that the most characteristic feature of structuralist criticism is a kind of transformation of form into content. It also accounts for the quotation marks that the word 'content' acquires in Eagleton's discussion, and underpins the conclusion of his illustration of structuralist method, with its echos of Jameson's observation:

> If the particular contents of the text are replaceable, there is a sense in which one can say that the 'content' of the narrative is its structure. This is equivalent to claiming that the narrative is in a way about itself:

> its 'subject' is its own internal relations, its own modes of sense-making.
>
> (1983: 96)

A minor qualification on this conclusion seems necessary. The available replacements of particular contents in a narrative are paradigms, and there is therefore a sense in which they are not 'internal relations'. They are rather relations between what is there in a narrative text and what is not there but could be. And as we have already seen, those paradigms are limited to the kind of replacements that preserve the structure of the narrative on the basis of their content. You can replace Eagleton's 'boy' with a 'mole', but not with a 'giant', or anything higher than its opposite. We might then want to conclude instead that the subject of a narrative is its own internal and external, syntagmatic and paradigmatic relations, and that the analysis does not succeed in banishing referential content (however it is understood) altogether.

What we are facing here is exactly the same ambiguity that presides over the concept of difference as an account of the linguistic sign: do the syntagmatic and paradigmatic relations between minimal units of a narrative merely enable, or actually constitute its content? Many available accounts of difference, of semiology and of literary structuralism give the impression, like Jameson and Eagleton, that the whole idea of content was swept aside by this kind of analysis. But the truth is a little more complicated; the question of referential meaning was never really settled, with the question of whether it was bracketed or displaced by structuralist analysis remaining unanswered.

Nevertheless this recasting of meaning in structural terms had an enormous impact on literary criticism in the middle of the twentieth century. In the previous section of this chapter I claimed that the poles of transparent and opaque language were often used as the basis for a distinction between prose and poetry, since the language and form of poetry is more visible, more bound up with its content. I also claimed that the distinction could be used to distinguish poetic types of prose from realist prose, which is more transparent. But what structuralist analysis shows is that even the content of the most transparent prose is inseparably bound to its form and structure, and this completely changes our framework for understanding the way that reference works. As Eagleton demonstrates, the structuralist method of reading a text displaces the idea of referential content as something extratextual, something outside of the text, with one in which referential content is embedded in a system or relations. Even if the status of the referent remained ambiguous and unsettled, the very dualistic framework for understanding reference, in literature and in general, in terms of form and content, or the inside and the outside of language, yielded to the more monistic view of form and content as categorically inseparable aspects of significance.

The concept of difference, elaborated as syntagmatic and paradigmatic relations, has delivered us to the gateway of what is now called post-structuralism. There were many linguists, philosophers and literary critics who realised that there was something unsettled in structuralist theory on the subject of referential meaning. In the work of Paul de Man, for example, we find the question of reference behind much of his criticism. According to de Man, the structuralist semiologists and the narratologists had gone some way towards freeing literary criticism from what he calls the 'debilitating burden of paraphrase' (de Man 1979: 5), but they had not gone far enough. In other words, the semiologists had done a lot to move criticism away from the idea that they had to represent what a text was about, to paraphrase its content, or to talk about it as if it represented a real world of people and events. But if, despite all the emphasis on the formal system of a narrative, the referential content has merely been bracketed, left aside or ignored, there is a sense in which it is still hovering over the analysis. De Man wants to move away from this towards a more radical critique of reference:

> [the] radical critique of referential meaning never implied that the referential function of language could in any way be avoided, bracketed, or reduced to being just one contingent property of language among others, as is postulated for example, in contemporary semiology.
>
> (1979: 204)

This is one way of understanding the nature of poststructuralist criticism: that even if structuralism had conflated the form and content, or the structure and the meaning of discourse to the extent that they could no longer be separated, there was a residual dualism, or a persistence of referential content, in their critical practice. It is, for example, easy to see that when a structuralist reduces a narrative to a series of propositions or minimal units, there is a kind of paraphrase at work. If I reduce *Pride and Prejudice* to an abstract schema (A is a woman; B is a man; B proposes to A; A declines; A learns that her impression of B is false; A and B marry) I am, however shoddily, paraphrasing its content. The particular contents (Elizabeth, Mr Darcy, etc.) are subtracted, but the idea of content has not been altogether banished. In *Allegories of Reading* de Man talks about this residual referential meaning in very negative terms, as a fiend that asserts itself 'in a variety of disguises', as a germ that requires some 'preventative semiological hygiene' and as a fallacy that actually prevents the critic from seeing the literariness of literature: '[Semiology] demonstrated that the perception of the literary dimension of language is largely obscured if one submits uncritically to the authority of reference' (1979: 5). This project to rid criticism once and for all of its concern with referential meaning is one way to understand the impact of poststructuralism, and leads to some interesting modifications of the concept of difference, which are discussed in the next chapter. It also helps to explain why, in the course of the twentieth century, critics went from writing sentences like this: 'When Elizabeth encounters Mr Darcy at the Netherfield ball, she is appalled at his character' to sentences like this: 'The aporia between perfomative and constative language is merely a version of the aporia between trope and persuasion that both generates and paralyses rhetoric.' In other words, it helps to explain how the concept of difference contributed to the utter transformation of critical discourse, from a mode of paraphrase to a linguistic jargon actively hostile to the content of a literary work.

3

DIFFERANCE

Differance, spelled with an 'a', is a notoriously unpindownable concept, but in fact it means something very close to 'unpindownability'. If so far we have had difference as the opposite of sameness, as the opposite of identity, the opposite of singularity and the opposite of reference, now, with the word 'differance', which Derrida claims is neither a word nor a concept at all, we are dealing with something like the opposite of presence, or even the opposite of concepthood. This chapter explains the connection between presence and concepthood, and why Derrida saw differance as their opposite, but it also explores some other poststructuralist approaches to and modifications of ideas about difference.

Most of the exposition in this chapter is theoretical and philosophical, and is based on the work of Derrida and Deleuze, two highly influential Parisian philosophers whose work in the second half of the twentieth century transformed criticism. Both Derrida and Deleuze are philosophers for whom literature (and art in general) has a special place, and indeed both are disinclined to draw a hard boundary between the discourses of philosophy and literature. If literature is a distinct kind of discourse for these philosophers, it is so because its language is not that of rigid truth-telling analysis. Literature, unlike traditional philosophy, deals in unpindownability, in fluidity and motion, and this elusive quality in literary language is something that Derrida and Deleuze, in different ways, have sought to incorporate in their own philosophical writing. There is a need in both writers to abandon the rigours of traditional philosophical style, the dominance of classical logic as the governing value of philosophical writing, and the accompanying pretence of objectivity. In this sense, they might be seen as literary philosophers. This blurring of the boundary between philosophy and literature is a major emphasis of deconstruction, the kind of literary criticism most closely associated with Derrida's work, one of the characteristics of which is to issue serious challenges to the traditional relationship between a literary and a critical text.

Anyone who has read a critical work, or been taught a critical method, and felt that it is doing violence to the work under analysis has, in a sense, felt the impulse that lies behind much deconstructive and poststructuralist criticism. Deconstruction as a kind of criticism can be roughly divided into two types. The first type is a kind of criticism that finds the most rigid and analytical approaches to literature unsatisfactory: too riddled with presuppositions, too partial in their use of evidence, too prepared to translate literature into something completely different, too distant from the nature of literature itself, and too sure of the truth of their own discoveries. A common strategy for this first type of deconstruction is to take a rigid analytical model (perhaps the search for unity in a work, or the ordered schematics of structuralist narratology) and show its failure to account for the complex, sometimes contradictory, often untidy multiplicity that is a literary work. The second type of deconstruction probably has similar aims, but sets about demonstrating the unpindownable excess of a literary work without engaging with a rigid analytical framework at all. The first type is an analytical approach to the destruction of analytical systems, while the second type is a playful, celebratory imitation of the literary object at its most chaotic; the first is rigorous, the second is ludic. In either case the deconstructive reading is intent on unravelling previous readings, especially those conveying a sense of the authority of their own interpretation.

Rigorous and ludic deconstruction share an important characteristic, which is that they refuse the traditional authority of a critical act whereby the analysis looks down on the literary object from an Olympian height, or a position of objective and scientific neutrality. The deconstructive reading always tries to locate itself inside its object, as far as that is possible, to avoid what Derrida calls the 'platitudes of a supposed academic meta-language', or the stupidity of thinking that a critic can stand back and speak the truth about language. For this reason – this refusal of analytical models, the rejection of the values of analytical distance – it is extremely difficult to illustrate in general terms what a deconstructive reading does to a literary text. Unlike structuralist narratology, deconstruction is not a method that can be applied to a literary text. And whereas the structuralist concept of difference is a linguistic analytical model that can be applied to almost anything, poststructuralist approaches to difference are mainly concerned to show that meaning can never be pinned down by such ordered systems. But even if deconstruction is not a method that can be applied, there are certain recurrent theoretical and logical problems that it attempts to expose and subvert in its dealings with literature and criticism. It is the purpose of this chapter to identify these recurrent issues and the kind of counter-strategies characteristically deployed in post-structuralist approaches to reading.

For the structuralist, the concept of difference lay at the heart of a scientific enterprise. It was a kind of foundation stone on top of which a highly systematic account of meaning was assembled. And yet there was always something about the concept of difference that militated against foundations, and therefore against the possibility of building stable structures on top of them. This paradox helps to characterise what have, in the Anglo-American world, come to be seen as poststructuralist developments in the concept of difference: developments that were concerned to pull away the foundation stone of structuralist science, and to watch the achievements of a systematic structural linguistics collapse. Or perhaps it would be more accurate to say that, for poststructuralists, the concept of difference produces insights that pull away its own foundation stone. This idea, that difference is self-subverting, or self-deconstructing, requires some explanation, but it is also important to say at the outset that this is not simply the end of the concept of difference; if anything it is the moment in the thinking through of difference where things get interesting. It may be a line of thought that heralds the end of difference as the basis of a systematic science, but it is also one that breathes new life into the concept of difference.

DIFFERENCE BEYOND OPPOSITIONS – DERRIDA

It will be clear from the last chapter, for example, that structuralism effectively imposed stability on the analysis of difference by focusing its attention on the simplest kind of difference: the binary opposition. But the binary opposition can only be seen as a stable meaning-generating unit when two antonymic signs are seen as if in isolation from the many other differences and relations that could be introduced into the analysis. To oversimplify the case for a moment, it could be said that the binary opposition was for people who could only count to two. For example, the idea that the meaning of the word 'day' inhered entirely in its relation to the word 'night' was somewhat reductive because it excluded consideration of the many gradations between night and day, excluded the difficult relations on the margin between them, such as dawn and dusk. To relate a word such as 'day' only to its antonym was to reduce difference to a single, determinable relation of the most simplified kind. One way of looking at the poststructuralist critique of structural linguistics is to see it as an opposition to this kind of simplistic reduction, as an attempt to acknowledge the complexity of a word's relations, or as a project to liberate difference from the closure of the binary opposition. The poststructuralist will for example speak of irreducible difference as a way of indicating the poverty of the dyad as the basic meaning-generating unit. Rather than accounting for the meaning of a word such as 'day' in relation to its opposite, the poststructuralist will characteristically focus on the borderline between the two signs, in the territory in which the difference between the two is less obviously oppositional and less clearly determinable. After structuralism there is a new interest in borderline territory, in margins, in zones of contestation between signs that defy the oppositional logic of the binary opposition.

It is probably immediately apparent that words and phrases like 'margins', 'borderlines' and 'zones of contestation' carry implications of social and political conflict, and such implications are an important part of the influence of poststructuralist thought. From the late 1960s onwards, there was a growing suspicion of the structuralist project to produce a neutral science of language and discourse, and an increasing imperative to analyse language in its relation to political history and political power. While much poststructuralist work does not explicitly address questions of history and politics, there is a clear movement in that direction, which can be discerned in the first place in terms suggesting a more politically engaged species of linguistic analysis. One area in which this is most apparent is exactly in a new direction in the analysis of binary opposition, which is no longer seen as an innocent structural relation but rather as a hierarchy. In Derrida's work, and in that of many literary and cultural critics who followed his ideas, there is always a sense that an opposition is no innocent structural relation but a power relation, in which one term dominates another. Even in the case of an opposition as apparently rooted in nature as night/day, there is a hierarchy which ascribes privilege, priority and positive value to one term at the expense of the other. Indeed the very idea of otherness comes to signify this power relation, this secondary and derivative position that one sign acquires in relation to another. And this dimension of an opposition is certainly not given in nature, but is actively produced in discourse, in the process of signification, or the way that signs are used. One need only think of the connotations of night and day, of what Derrida refers to as chains of connotation and associative links to recognise that day has a kind of priority over night, a privilege and priority that makes their relation far from symmetrical and allows day to be associated with life, knowledge, truth, purity and goodness while night connotes death, ignorance, corruption and evil. It is very often only by exploring the potential of signs as images, associations and suggestions that a hierarchy between the terms of a dyad is perceptible, and this points to an important development away from the supposedly value-free, scientific project of structural linguistics. Poststructuralist approaches to the binary opposition produce a kind of critique that unmasks power relations, that seeks to expose hierarchy, that refuses to isolate the sign from the discourse in which it operates, or for that matter that refuses to isolate the opposition from the more general discursive context in which its associative and suggestive potential is formed. If we take these two developments together, the liberation of difference from opposition on one hand, and a kind of critique that exposes hierarchy as it operates in discourse, we have a useful preliminary account of the characteristics of what came to be known, in the 1970s, as deconstruction.

In *Positions* (1981), Derrida describes deconstruction's approach to binary opposition as having three phases. The first phase is the exposure of a hierarchy, of the assumed superiority of one term over the other; the second phase is the reversal of that hierarchy, that is, the promotion of the secondary and derivative term to the position of superiority for strategic reasons; and the third phase is the reinscription of that opposition, which involves the disruption or reconfiguration of the difference between the two terms. There is nothing that Derrida abhors more vehemently than the idea that deconstruction might become some kind of analytical programme of easily assimilable and applicable techniques, and this is the closest he comes anywhere to a systematic account of the deconstructive approach to oppositions. Even if we respect Derrida's reluctance to systematise deconstruction, this account of the three phases of deconstruction provides an illuminating description of what takes place when he reads a text.

A now famous example of this strategy of reading comes from *Of Grammatology*, where Derrida takes Saussure's treatment of the opposition between speech and writing in the *Course in General Linguistics*. In a sense, this is an extreme example. Saussure's text does not subtly valorise speech over writing through associative or imagistic suggestivity. Rather he declares openly that writing is a secondary and derived kind of language, that it is merely the representation of speech, and therefore that it is to be banished: the proper object of linguistic study, says Saussure, is speech. There is therefore an explicit and unmistakable privilege assigned to speech over writing, and because it is so explicit, it serves as a particularly clear example of the deconstructive strategy that Derrida describes in *Positions*. Derrida argues that this privilege is nothing more than an inherited prejudice that has its basis in two presuppositions that Saussure receives uncritically from the tradition of thought about the nature of language. The first presupposition is that speech has a conceptual priority over writing because it has temporal priority over writing, which is to say that it comes first either in the history of language or in the acquisition of language in childhood. The second presupposition is closely related to the first, namely that speech is accorded this conceptual priority not only by virtue of coming before writing in time, but in being seen somehow as closer to the presence of meaning. In *Of Grammatology*, Derrida diagnoses this assumption as an unscientific ascription of value to speech on the basis of two different types of presence: the presence of signifying intention and the presence of the referent. In other words, the spoken sign is said to stand in a closer relation to the mind of the person who utters it, or to the thing or concept in the place of which the sign stands than the written sign. Indeed the written sign is conventionally understood as a kind of technology which works exactly by allowing language to circulate without the person or the referent any longer being present.

Here, then, we have an extreme case of an opposition working as a conceptual hierarchy, where that hierarchy is founded on unargued notions of presence and the priority that presence gives to language in its so-called original form over the secondary and derived technology that records speech as writing. This argument corresponds to the first phase of deconstruction in which a hierarchical opposition is identified. The second phase of the strategy is to invert this hierarchy, and to promote the inferior term to the position of privilege and dominance. In this case that involves the perhaps counter-intuitive suggestion that writing is in fact the truest nature of language. It should be pointed out that this paraphrase is something of a heresy for two reasons. The first is that Derrida does not generally offer metalingual propositions of this kind in a way that allows their extraction from the reading of a particular text. Deconstruction in its strictest philosophical sense almost always involves the demonstration that a text somehow contains a counter-suggestion to its own presuppositions or its own declared positions: that it subverts its own theses and beliefs. The second is that Derrida does not really claim that there is something truer about writing than speech. Instead he shows that when Saussure tries to explain the innermost workings of spoken language, he resorts to an analogy with written language, using the banished and secondary term to explain the nature of the privileged and prior term. The inversion of the hierarchy is therefore not proposed by Derrida from the outside, but is located within the argument that exactly seeks to establish that hierarchy. In this way, Derrida demonstrates that Saussure's attempt to reduce writing to a secondary status is subverted by the fact that he also resorts to the example of writing, exactly for its ability to circulate in the absence of the referent and the signifying intention, to illustrate the innermost workings of speech. As he teases out this counter-suggestion from Saussure's text, his own establishes that writing is just as capable of occupying the dominant position in the hierarchy. This leads us to the third phase of deconstruction, the reinscription of the opposition, which in this case consists in the conflation of the terms 'speech' and 'writing' as what Derrida calls 'Arche-writing', or to put it another way, the temporal priority of speech over writing is reconfigured with writing as the origin, so that the very opposition of origin and supplement breaks down.

What does this have to do with the concept of difference? The first answer to this question is that the binary opposition, which for the structuralist was a kind of unit of difference, is now a rather unreliable basis for the explanation of how significance is generated. In this kind of argument the opposition is something closer to the problem than the solution: the mask rather than the unmasker. But there is a second implication in this for the concept of difference, which helps to explain Derrida's resistance to the structuralist concept of difference. In the example of the opposition of speech and writing, speech is understood as that which comes first and writing that which follows from it, speech as the origin and writing as the supplement. This temporal difference, the temporal dimension of an opposition has a special place in Derrida's thought and is of particular importance for the understanding of Derrida's critique of the notion of difference which is implicit in his own modified version of the term. Differance has become known as Derrida's little graphic joke. It is the modification of the concept of difference which cannot be heard (since the words difference and differance sound the same, especially in the original French), which asserts the written over the spoken, and which carries within it a critique of the atemporal nature of the structuralist concept of difference. Derrida's line of argument about speech and writing, about the presupposition of presence in speech where speech is the origin of writing, is best understood in relation to the term 'differance'.

According to Derrida, differance is neither a word nor a concept, which is to say that it is not a free-standing notion which can be extracted and applied to the analysis of texts in the way that difference perhaps could be. Rather it is a term that names a problem in the former concept of difference. The argument of the last chapter shows that the structuralist concept of difference aimed to show that a word could never be viewed as a free-standing entity but rather has to be articulated into the system of differences which underlie its meaning. The term 'differance' might be viewed as an attempt to redouble this insight into the dependence of a word on different terms which are not present. But whereas structuralism tended to freeze the language system into a synchronic snapshot, a spatial structure, Derrida aims to point to a set of dependencies or relations across time. The term 'differance' therefore carries within it not only the structural relations of a word to a stable language system, but the temporal relations of a word to those that precede it and follow it.

This is the main sense in which differance can be understood as a critique of difference: it functioned as a criticism of the synchronic orientation of structuralist analysis. The Saussurean model of the sign had dictated that meaning be analysed as a spatial structure, where the language system is frozen in time and viewed as a structural whole. It was a common perception that this banished time and history entirely from structuralist analysis, and yet it doesn't take much exploration in, for example, works of structuralist narratology to determine that the internal temporality of a narrative – the order and frequency of its events – was one of the major concerns of the structuralists. Nor was it ahistorical in itself to take such a snapshot of the language system, since in theory at least, that might involve reconstructing the system of conventions, oppositions and codes as a kind of linguistic-historical context for any given utterance. In practice, however, there were few structuralist linguists who would go to the trouble of reconstructing the system of antonyms and synonyms that would give a sign its meaning at the time of its utterance or point out historical differences between the system at the time of the text's production and the time of its analysis. In theory there may have been an interest in narrative time, but in practice the potential historical dimension of synchronic analysis was generally disregarded. Even the structuralist narratologist's interest in temporality was somewhat misleading in that the internal, temporal sequence of narrative was seen as a spatial or structural organisation of narrative elements. In theory, structuralist narratology was neither ahistorical nor uninterested in the temporal organisation of narrative, but in practice anything temporal was quickly translated into spatial relationships or differences.

In this context, the Derridean concept of differance, with its temporal and spatial meanings, can be understood as an attempt to think about difference and time at the same time, and therefore to allow a temporal dimension back into the analysis of language. As the last chapter illustrated, the structural analysis of a sentence, or a narrative, would look at syntagmatic relations between the components of the sequence, or the relationship between any sign and the sentence as a whole, as if these were stable structural relations. The model of differance, on the other hand, implied that the relationships between the elements of a sentence were always in motion, or that the meaning of any sign was always qualifying those preceding it in the sequence or waiting to be qualified by those that followed. This is what Derrida referred to as the *trace* structure of the sign: that any sign is embedded in a context, and that its meaning bears the trace of the signs that surround it, that have preceded it, and that follow it. The sign was seen by the structuralist as an entity that was not complete in itself because it was partly defined by relations with other signs in the language system. What is being said here is that this is also true of other signs in a sentence, or sequence of signs. But these other signs are not exactly co-present, as structuralism had seen it. They are in the past and still to come, so that the meaning of any sign is partly comprised by elements of the past and the future. The meaning of a sign is therefore not complete in itself, or is not present within itself, but somehow spread out across all the others. Nor is there any limit to the dissemination of meaning across other signs. Derrida talks of meaning as having no respite in the 'indefinite referral from signifier to signifier' (1978: 25) because the model of differance posits that neither the beginning nor ends of a sentence or a book can stop this movement.

Again, this is an apparently simple observation which Derrida manages to amplify, until the trace structure of the sign becomes the basis for the deconstruction of the concept of time itself:

> The concepts of present, past and future, everything in the concepts of time and history which implies evidence of them – the metaphysical concept of time in general – cannot adequately describe the structure of the trace. And deconstructing the simplicity of presence does not amount to accounting for the horizons of potential presence, indeed of a dialectic of protension and retension that one would install in the heart of the present instead of surrounding it with it.
>
> (1976: 67)

Much of Derrida's thought takes the position that linguistic meaning, time and history are suggestively linked in this way, and this phrase – 'a dialectic of protension and retension that one would install in the heart of the present' – makes it clear why. *Protensions* and *retensions* are simply hints of the future and traces of the past which, he argues, the present is constituted by. When Derrida refers to the metaphysical concepts of meaning, time or history he is drawing attention to this foundational illusion of presence, which is destroyed by these traces, that is, it is destroyed by the fact that the present, or presence itself, is a crossed structure of protensions and retensions, bearing within it the spectres of its own past and future. If time and history are being readmitted here it is in an unrecognisable form, which destroys the linear sequence of past, present and future with the logic of the trace and understands the components of any sequence as constitutive of each other. As I said at the outset of the chapter, this is perhaps the simplest way of defining differance: that it is the opposite of presence, or perhaps that it is the name of the non-existence of presence.

It is difficult then to say that the concept of differance, with its temporal dimension, justified a straighforward return to historicism. Because literary criticism, particularly in the United States, was always polarised and polemicised around the opposition between political criticism (committed to historicism) and a depoliticised formalism, there was some confusion about what this kind of argument represented for critical practice. It seemed to be disturbing the simplicities of formalism with the complexities of time, which had been so strictly excluded from structuralism, and yet it also seemed to be disrupting the simplicities of time with a formal argument about the relations between the signifiers in any chain. It remained unclear, however, what a non-metaphysical approach to time would look like, and even less clear how historical writing could base itself on such an approach.

Derrida makes some attempt to clarify this issue in *Positions*, which was enormously influential in the United States. Resistance to the metaphysical concept of history, he claims, would involve resistance to both 'history in general and the general concept of history'. In the case of the former, the resistance to 'history in general' might involve subscribing to something like Althusser's critique of Hegel's concept of history, which 'aims to show that there is not one single history, but rather histories different in their type, rhythm, mode of inscription – intervallic, differentiated histories' (1973: 58). It certainly sounds as if this rejection of a single, general history was politically motivated, and would therefore offer deconstruction as a resource to those political critics for whom historicisation was a critical imperative. However the rejection of the 'general concept of history' was less obviously so, and seemed to amount to little more than a view that histories differed from each other, or that it would be a mistake to assume that there was any kernel, any common denominator that might link different histories together. If such a common denominator had been assumed by traditional historians, it is, in Derrida's account, the assumption of linearity: the implication that one thing leads to another, which supports 'an entire system of implications (teleology, eschatology, elevating and interiorizing accumulation of meaning, a certain type of traditionality, a certain concept of continuity, of truth, etc.)' (1973: 57). Whereas the first argument seems to encourage the writing of more histories – the histories of those excluded by history in general for example – the second seems to undermine completely what we think of as, and how we might write, history. These issues are of great importance for literary criticism because they underpin ideas about the pluralism of history as well as raise questions about narrative linearity, issues lying at the heart of criticism as well as fiction, drama and poetry, which will be explored more fully in chapter 4.

The importance of this argument is the connection it established between the linearity of narrative and the metaphysics of presence, against which Derrida pitches the counter-strategy of differance, that is, of time understood as differance. Because for Derrida presence is a spatio-temporal category (in that it has both spatial and temporal meanings), one way of explaining the temporalised meaning of differance is through the spatial or structural sense of difference that has already been discussed: the view of the sign that attempts to exclude or repress its differences. For Derrida, the sign was a structure of exclusion. The whole idea of the sign as a carrier of meaning was based on the principle that its meaning could be fenced off from other meanings. Saussure may have argued that it was the differences between signs that enabled them to signify, but he did not go as far as to say that the meaning of a sign was actually constituted by those differences. Even in the radical terms of structural linguistics there is a sense that the meaning of a sign is pure. The sign is not internally divided. It is surrounded by difference but not contaminated by difference. Derrida's account of the sign can be summarised as an opposition to this idea of the pure self-identical sign, to show that the sign is always internally divided, different from itself.

As I said in Chapter 1, a sign then represses difference in two distinct ways. The first is that, like the word 'history', the sign always posits some common denominator, some sameness between the things that it denominates, so that the word 'dog' posits a common essence between dogs, which represses the differences between dogs. The second is that the sign represses the differences between dogs and cats, because every time that 'dog' presents itself as an apparently autonomous word, it hides or excludes the other words from which it differs, pretending that its meaning is constituted by itself and not by difference. We might now add a third way in which the sign represses difference. It represses the temporal differences between itself and the other signs in the sequence in which it is embedded.

My aim here, and in the following chapter, is to show that these notions about the sign as a structure of exclusion act as a kind of foundation for most of the political criticism of the last decade, which characteristically argues at the level of discourse that what is not there in a discourse is constitutive of what is. For the moment I want to digress for the sake of further illustration of the third kind of repression of difference. For linguists, the word is the 'minimum free form', which means that it is the smallest linguistic unit that can be taken out of its context, used in another, and still mean the same thing. This makes the word different from the phoneme, since the phoneme doesn't have meaning on its own. It must be combined with other phonemes into a word for meaning to occur. In other words, the meaning of a phoneme is context-bound whereas the meaning of a word is free. This is the traditional view that Derrida's differance challenges. One of the many jokes contained in the word 'differance' is that one little phonemic change, a phonemic change that cannot even be heard, can alter the meaning of the word 'difference' from a structural to a temporal relation. This tiny change highlights a principle with large consequences for narrative thought in general. Not only are words internally divided by an alterable sequence of letters with an individual potential to disrupt meaning. The meaning of a word is also context-bound in the sense that it bears the trace of other words in the sequence to which it belongs. Like the phoneme it is only as part of a combinative sequence that the word accrues meaning, so that it is marked by the temporal process of the discourse it is part of. And it is marked by the trace of words that are not part of the discourse at hand, but that (like the paradigmatic relations of structuralism) are ghostly absences inhabiting the word. What all these factors conspire to show is that a word is not simply a free form or the bearer of meaning as presence, since that presence is always contaminated by absences, traces of context, both immediate and distant.

A concept as apparently innocent as the 'minimum free form' turns out to be a multidimensional repression of difference, a structure of exclusion, which seeks to establish hard and fast boundaries around its meaning as if that meaning were not marked by protensions and retensions of other signs in the discourse, and of former and future discourses. What happens when this principle of the trace is scaled up to the level of a sentence, a narrative episode, or an entire discourse? One answer is that the attempt to isolate any larger discursive unit and repress the trace of differences within it gives the concepts of autonomy, purity and presence a discernibly political importance, where the assumed linearity of a discourse can be seen as an agent of particular ideological bent. Two examples of the structure of exclusion at this level, and the role of narrative linearity in the repression of difference are the critique of origins and the critique of 'positivist history' (best understood in this context as history dominated by cause and effect, and therefore by narrative linearity), both of which begin to clarify the link between these purely structural arguments about the constitution of a word, and the temporal version of the structure of exclusion.

One of the obvious consequences of this kind of argument – that the word cannot be extracted from the *process* of language, or that it is always marked by the past and future – is that there can be no such thing as a moment. A moment, like a word, only comes into being as a structure of exclusion or an undivided presence. A moment can only be present when it is not yet in the past and no longer in the future. But any definition of what a moment is, any attempt to cleanse the moment of the trace of past and future and see it as pure presence, will be forced to impose arbitrary boundaries to mark off the present from past and future. As with any structure of exclusion, the moment then becomes an entity in its own right but only by virtue of the fact that it has arbitrarily excluded the relations that constitute it. One is hard pushed to explain what one means by 'a moment' without reference to the past and the future because it is structured by their exclusion. According to Derrida, the elusive nature of the moment is like the elusive nature of undivided presence in general. Its autonomy or purity is mythical. It is a desire rather than an actuality. One reason that undivided presence can be understood as a desire is that it helps to bring the explanation of something to rest on something stable, something no longer in motion, no longer referring backwards or waiting to be altered.

The desire for presence helps to explain what Derrida means when he talks about *metaphysical* history. Metaphysics for Derrida is the metaphysics of presence, any science of presence, so that metaphysical history is any history that sees the passage of time as a sequence of present moments, any one of which can be isolated from the sequence and seen in terms of this mythical purity and presence. It also helps to explain why Derrida devotes so much of his writing to the deconstruction of origins. An origin is the first moment in a historical sequence. It is, in a sense, an easier moment to mythologise as presence because nothing comes before it, and at the time it occurs, it has not yet been marked by subsequent moments. This means that when you want to explain something, its origin is a useful bedrock for the explanation. An explanation will often narrate the history of that something from the point of originary purity and self-presence, often as a fall from that original state of presence. At one level the sign itself is a fall from presence, since it can be circulated, repeated and used without the thing to which it refers being present. Interpreting the sign then becomes a process of working backwards to the originary and mythical moment when the sign and the thing were unified, when the meaning of the sign was present. Writing is also a fall from presence since like the sign it is exterior to what it means, capable of signifying in the absence of the writer, creating a kind of nostalgia for its origin, the moment when the mind that produced it was present, when it was full with signifying intention, or when it was speech. Speech is also the origin of writing in the sense that it comes first, in childhood, or in the history of humankind, and this temporal priority is often seen as a kind of logical or metaphysical priority. To explain writing, it then becomes necessary to trace it back to its origin in speech, where language can be seen in its purest form. Driven by desire for presence, all such explanations, whether about language or not, are targets for deconstruction.

Whether it is the desire to see meaning as contained in a minimum free form, stabilised in structural terms, grounded in a present moment, underpinned by an origin or purified of difference, these are all strategies of thought that attempt to pin meaning down to something determinable. And differance is a kind of force at work in language, a state of motion or process making it impossible to do so. It is in this sense that presence, meaning and concepthood are not only linked, but are all equally unpindownable. We might say then that the unpindownability of an origin is exactly what supplementarity names, since supplementarity is a logic in which the primacy of an origin is simply rejected: 'The strange structure of the supplement appears here: by delayed reaction, a possibility produces that to which it is said to be added on' (Derrida 1973: 89). If differance is the unstoppability of time and the unpindownability of meaning, supplementarity might be thought of as a subset or an example of differance, in which the origin becomes contaminated by protensions of the future.

What we are looking at here, in the term 'differance', or the logic of supplementarity, is a cluster of problems that transforms the structuralist approach to difference. As I have suggested, some of these problems (the critique of metaphysical time, the idea of narrative as a structure of exclusion) are particularly important for developments in historicist criticism, and in many ways underpin the critical practices of new historicism, cultural materialism, feminism and psychoanalysis, though by now it will be clear that 'underpin' is not the most appropriate metaphor. These connections will be developed in the following chapters. For the moment I want to look beyond Derrida to other poststructuralist thinkers whose treatment of the term 'difference' contributes to its evolution away from the systematic and scientific orientation of structural linguistics.

DIFFERENCE AND REPETITION – DELEUZE

It is now possible to characterise a poststructuralist concept of difference in a series of propositions: (1) a word is constituted by temporal as well as spatial differences; (2) a word is no more extractable from a sequence than is a phoneme; (3) a binary opposition is not flat but hierarchical; (4) a hierarchical opposition has a temporal dimension which assigns privilege to origins or endpoints; (5) the presence of meaning is an illusion constructed by the exclusion of spatial and temporal differences. What these propositions amount to is something quite unruly. No longer can a sign be seen as an entity in its own right, an entity that is stable, or belongs in a stable structure that provides the basis of its intelligibility. According to the counter-logic of differance, language is in motion, and difference is at play. The sense in many poststructuralist conceptions of difference is that opposition has always been a way of constricting difference to a single relation, and therefore confining difference and multiplicity to prevent its play: 'Opposition ceases its labour and difference begins its play', as Gilles Deleuze puts it in *Difference and Repetition*.

Deleuze is perhaps the most substantial philosopher of difference of the twentieth century. Like Derrida, his concept of difference is not one that begins with Saussure but is rooted in a longer tradition of philosophers of difference such as Kant, Hegel, Nietzsche, Bergson and Heidegger. It would be beyond my powers of exposition to summarise this tradition, but it is undoubtedly worthwhile to look at some of the ways in which Deleuze formulates the concept of difference and adds to its power as a critical concept. The pursuit for Deleuze is what he calls a true philosophy of difference, which entails finding a way of thinking about difference that does not simply draw the meaning of difference from its opposition with identity. The problem here is that difference is easily conceived as a kind of division of something singular and self-identical, as the identification of species within a genus, in such a way that difference cannot be asserted without at the same time implying the existence of identity, of the undivided. For Deleuze, difference is too often thought of as the inferior member in an opposition with the concept of identity. If Derrida understood the whole project of philosophy as a quest for foundational moments of presence, Deleuze has a similar concern with the idea that philosophy can represent stable identities, or with the idea of the representation of concepts in general. In *Difference and Repetition*, first published in Paris in 1968, he sets out the arguments that oppose difference to representation in general, on the grounds that representation is the logic of mediating identities as static entities. Most important in this set of arguments is the necessity to upturn the established hierarchy between identity and difference, to see difference as the principle that underlies identity, and furthermore, to understand difference as a kind of ever-shifting ground behind everything rather than as the mere division or multiplication of identities:

> The immediate, defined as 'sub-representative', is therefore not attained by multiplying representations and points of view. On the contrary, each composing representation must be distorted, diverted and torn from its centre. Each point of view must itself be the object, or the object must belong to the point of view. The object must therefore in no way be identical, but torn asunder in a difference in which the identity of the object as seen by a seeing subject vanishes. Difference must become the element, the ultimate unity; it must therefore refer to other differences which never identify it but rather differentiate it. Each term in a series, being already a difference, must be put into a variable relation with other terms, thereby constituting other series devoid of centre and convergence. Divergence and decentering must be affirmed in the series itself. Every object, every thing must see its own identity swallowed up in difference, each being no more than a difference between differences. Difference must be shown differing.
>
> (1994: 56)

It is clear here that difference must never be allowed to return to the concept of identity as a source of stability or stasis. Rather, the aim for philosophy is movement. Philosophy must point to the unceasing movement of difference, to the impossibility of arresting movement in any kind of stable centre. Perhaps the most interesting thing about this passage from *Difference and Repetition* is that it helps to clarify the ways in which poststructuralist conceptions of difference might actually inform criticism or an understanding of art and literature. Both before and after this passage, Deleuze points to art as places where this kind of unstoppable motion are experienced. If Derrida's notion of differance was a move towards a rather chaotic conception of the coexistence of moments, this is exactly Deleuze's motivation in introducing movement into philosophy:

> Movement, for its part, implies a plurality of centres, a superimposition of perspectives, a tangle of points of view, a co-existence of moments

which essentially distort representation: paintings or sculptures are already such 'distorters', forcing us to create movement.

(1994: 56)

And the paragraph concludes with an account of the role of art in introducing movement as a distortion of representation:

We know that modern art tends to realise these conditions: in this sense it becomes a veritable *theatre* of metamorphoses and permutations. A theatre where nothing is fixed, a labyrinth without a thread (Ariadne has hung herself). The work of art leaves the domain of representation in order to become 'experience', transcendental empiricism or science of the sensible.

(1994: 56)

Here, Deleuze does something that can be thought of as a characteristic poststructuralist manoeuvre. He accords to modern art an already established philosophical import. In a move that can be found repeatedly in the work of Derrida and Paul de Man, he locates in art and literature a philosophical potential to distort representation, to convey movement, flux and multiplicity that cannot be found in traditional philosophical writing. According to this view, the purpose of philosophy and criticism would not be to mediate, represent, analyse or explain art and literature but to acknowledge its superiority precisely as a philosophy of movement, a transcendental empiricism, or a science of the sensible.

To the literary critic, let us say a literary critic, turning to Deleuze for some enhanced knowledge of literature, this might seem a rather unpromising direction. It seems to be saying that when a work of art is still, such as sculpture or painting, we are forced to provide movement, and when it is in movement we must recognise its superiority to the stasis of traditional philosophy. In the relationship between literature and criticism, criticism would then be understood as a rather foolish attempt to impose stability on the theatre of metamorphoses and permutations that is literature. Criticism would indeed only be fulfilling its function when it exists to tease out this knowledge of multiplicity and movement from the texts it analyses. If this seems a negative characterisation of the function of criticism, it is certainly not conceived as such by Deleuze, whose writing constantly turns towards the notion of the affirmation of difference. If we think back to the structuralist application of the concept of difference to literature, we will remember that the binary opposition was seen there as a fundamental linguistic unit as well as a structural principle for literary texts. But in the work of Derrida and Deleuze, the rejection of the binary opposition is based in the view that the opposition is not something operating in language and literature so much as something brought to it by the analysis of language and literature. The binary opposition is a limited framework according to which a literary text is constructed by the critic, rather than a logic governing the production of literature. Here we have a significant shift which characterises much deconstructive thinking about literature. No longer is structure seen as a straightforwardly objective property of a text under analysis, or indeed of the language system at large. Structure is rather something that is projected on to the object by the analysis itself. Critical analysis is therefore a process of invention rather than a discovery of inherent properties, an act of structuration rather than a science of structure. This points to a highly significant change in the relationship between the literary and the critical text, which it is possible, with Deleuze, to view in the most positive terms. If structuralism tended to constrict the object of analysis by construing it according to the strictures of the binary opposition, poststructuralism prefers to free it again by demonstrating the complex motion that such analyses attempt to arrest. This is certainly an emphasis typical of deconstruction: that it generally aims to untie some over-schematic system for analysis by celebrating the elusive motion of the object that it purports to analyse.

For Deleuze, celebration is not an inappropriate word, since he regards the emphasis placed on opposition in a metalanguage such as linguistics as a particularly negative mindset. Opposition, after all, locates sigificance in a relation between any given term and its negative, and when 'difference is read as opposition, it is deprived of the peculiar thickness in which its positivity is affirmed' (1994: 205). And it is this reduction of difference to opposition that defines Deleuze's position not only in relation to structuralism, but also to Hegelian dialectical thinking. Why, he asks, 'does Saussure, at the very moment when he discovers that "in language there are only differences" add that these differences are "without positive terms" and "eternally negative"?' And equally he claims that a Hegelian (meaning a philosopher concerned with dialectics and contradictions, and therefore with binary oppositions) feels ill at ease in a 'complex or perplexed differential mechanism . . . in the absence of the uniformity of a large contradiction' (1994: 204). Opposition and contradiction are, according to Deleuze, equally negative ways of reducing difference, against which the notion of difference as a positive multiplicity must be asserted:

> It seems to us that pluralism is a more enticing and dangerous thought: fragmentation implies overturning. The discovery in any domain of a plurality of co-existing oppositions is inseparable from a more profound discovery, that of difference which denounces the negative and opposition itself as no more than appearances in relation to the problematic field of a positive multiplicity. One cannot pluralise opposition without leaving its domain and entering the caves of difference which resonate a pure positivity and reject opposition as no more than a shadow cavern seen from without.
>
> (1994: 204)

Of course there have been those, and I am thinking here mainly of Alan Badiou (2000), who might be thought of as one of Deleuze's philosophical opponents in Paris, who have pointed out Deleuze's own dependence on analytical and hierarchical oppositions such as inside and outside, singular and plural, active and passive, positive and negative and not least, opposition and difference. It should be said in his defence that *Difference and Repetition* is his most schematic, manifesto-like statement of the philosophy of difference, which does lapse into a kind of performative contradiction, of saying one thing while doing another. Elsewhere, and particularly in his writings on literature and cinema, there is a greater sense that his own writing practice affirms difference without recourse to the kind of analytical opposition that is clearly at work in the passage above. In such cases, Deleuze's work comes closer to Derrida's careful avoidance of the opposition as a framework for reading, or to a critical practice that constantly affirms the contamination of presence.

4

DIFFERENT HISTORIES

In the 1980s and 1990s critics and theorists began to think about history in a different way, and at the same time, critics and writers actually began to rewrite history from many different points of view. Of course, the understanding of history had by no means been stable up to this point, and there is a sense in which history is constantly rewritten from the point of view of the present. But for literary criticism, this return to history, to new and different histories, represented a significant change of direction: away from the various kinds of formalist criticism that dominated in earlier decades of the twentieth century. There are two different ways in which the concept of difference contributed to these processes. The first was by writing history in a different way, on the basis of a more complex view of time of the kind outlined in the previous chapter in relation to poststructuralist ideas of difference. The second was by introducing the idea of cultural difference, differences of class, race and gender, for example, or identities that had traditionally been excluded from history. This chapter is about the way that these two types of difference can be considered together, and the way that together they transformed the writing of history.

The previous chapter focused on the introduction of time into difference, and much of its argument is relevant to the way that literary critics dealt with the question of history in the 1980s and 1990s. It is a widely held view that Derrida's work represents a kind of assault on the pre-suppositions of historical knowledge, or that it somehow places in question the very possibility of historical knowledge. But this is not a simple issue. It can, for example, be surprising to revisit critical journals in the United States in the early 1970s for the extent to which they contradict this view. In these early days of the reception of Derrida's work in the United States, there is a clear sense of possibility that Derrida might provide for the return of historicism in literary criticism. It is easy to see why. American criticism had been predominantly formalist through most of the twentieth century, with historicism relegated to a position of polemical counter-argument. In the 1960s, the somewhat ahistorical tendencies of the New Criticism were coming to share critical territory with the more rigorous and systematic formalisms associated with Northrop Frye and the imported French structuralists. The concept of difference, therefore, carried with it the threat of an increasingly anti-historicist inclination, underpinned as it was by the synchronic (or 'snapshot') method derived from Saussurean linguistics. Derrida's concept of differance, as I have shown, reintroduces a temporal dimension to the concept of difference, and therefore seemed to offer the historicist critic a faint prospect of escape from the snapshot of synchronicity.

In addition to the apparent temporality of differance, there was also the influence of *Positions*, Derrida's collection of plain-speaking interviews, in which he makes clear that it is only a metaphysical concept of history that is the butt of his critique. In other words, while some historicist suppositions – the view of history as a succession of present moments, the idea of a single general history, the idea that there might be common denominators that link different histories together, the idea of continuity in history – are placed in question, the possibility of writing history in such a way that does not fall into such assumptions remains open. It was clear in the previous chapter that there are ways of privileging, or mythologising, certain moments such as origins and endpoints which will have implications for the way that history is written. These patterns, which might be called *genetic* (meaning concerned with beginnings) and *teleological* (meaning concerned with endpoints) histories, are at odds with the logic of differance, or the logic of supplementarity, which aim to do justice to the cross-contamination of moments in any temporal sequence. One of the general characteristics of poststructuralist criticism is that it aims to write history differently, and particularly through an awareness of the cross-contamination between the past that is being described and the present moment from which it is being described. I have argued that the poststruturalist critique of linguistics conflated the language being described with the metalanguage describing it, so that structures and differences are seen as properties of the subject just as much as of the object of analysis. The same kind of conflation of the subject and object presides over the critique of historicism. If the object of historical knowledge is the past, the poststructuralist critic seeks to emphasise that the writing of history is the active structuration of that past from the present: an act in which the pastness of the past is inevitably contaminated by the present from which it is described. This might seem like a straight-forward problem, or one well known to every student of history, but it can also be argued that its full implications have, only relatively recently, been incorporated into the practice of historicist writing or adequately theorised in terms of subject–object relations. If, for example, Derrida has at times been misunderstood as an anti-historicist, or an apolitical thinker, there has been a more recent recognition, or revival of the view that his work presents new historicist and political possibilities. Kiernan Ryan, a commentator on and practitioner of the new historicisms, is one who gets the emphasis right:

> Being cast adrift forever on the shoreless seas of textuality does have its advantages, however. The empirical materiality of history may have vanished, but at least all the old metaphysical ideas of history have vanished along with it, including the notion of history as 'background' or as the bedrock reality that literature subsequently mirrors or misrepresents.

(1996: 4)

Catherine Belsey (1998) is another who recognises the contribution that Derrida, alongside Michel Foucault, makes to 'a mode of history which is profoundly political'. This chapter aims to illustrate, therefore, that the ideas expounded in the previous chapter, of differance, structures of exclusion, and the poststructuralist critique of metaphysical history, provide the new unstable ground on which a different kind of history is written.

THE CROSS-CONTAMINATION OF SUBJECT
AND OBJECT IN HISTORICAL KNOWLEDGE

A simple approach to the problem of the cross-contamination of past and present, subject and object, would be to see the two poles as a kind of contradiction or paradox. How can it be claimed at the same time that historicism can know the past as past and yet view the pastness of the past as an invention in the present? One answer to this would be that it is a bit of both, that the subject and object, the present and past, exist only in a contradictory and dialectical relation with each other. It might then be possible to go on writing history, or being historicist, while sustaining an awareness that the past is inevitably tinged with the present, and being content to live with the contradiction. Deleuze however is not content with this solution because, for him, difference is always more complex than mere opposition. This is the basis for much of Deleuze's disagreement with Hegel, whose work he sees as limited by the idea that contradiction is 'the absolute maximum of difference'. Hegel, claims Deleuze, criticises his predecessors on the grounds that 'they stopped at a purely relative maximum without reaching the absolute maximum of difference, namely contradiction; they stopped before reaching the infinite (as infinitely large) of contradiction' (1994: 44). But according to Deleuze it is a mistake to determine the maximum of difference by the opposition of extremes or contraries. He argues that this idea of the infinite 'entails the identity of contraries', and therefore that the power of difference remains contained by opposition, within the orbit of the concept of identity. This line of critique is part of a complex argument that the importance of the concept of difference, its power to disrupt the concept of identity, is diminished by the Hegelian notion of contradiction, since contradiction as the maximum of difference is a rather crude framework in which to understand identity. Deleuze infinitely prefers what he sees as a Leibnizian idea of 'infinitely small difference', that is, in the place of the crude opposition he prefers a more subtle sense of fine gradations and minor nuances of difference. If we return to the question of the relation of present and past, therefore, it follows that the solution to the paradox of present subject and past object cannot be provided, to Deleuze's satisfaction, by the dialectical view that historical knowledge is somehow comprised of both things. To do so is merely to replace the identity of the past with the identity of two things: the past and the present.

When Deleuze turns his attention to the knowability of the past, then, we find him looking for something more complex than contradiction, or something more differentiated than mere opposition. He finds inspiration for this more complex schema in the work of Henri-Louis Bergson (1859–1941), whose paradoxes about time provide Deleuze with a kind of matrix of paradoxes. There are, Deleuze argues, at least two presents involved in the notion of the past: the present present in relation to which the past is past, and the former present, which is not the same thing as the past, since the past is only the element that we now focus on from the new present. The past then cannot be seen as the same thing as the former present, because in the former present it wasn't yet passed. 'The present and former presents are not', he argues, 'like two successive instants on the line of time; rather the present one necessarily contains an extra dimension in which it represents the former and also represents itself' (1994: 80). The first paradox then results from this inescapable doubleness:

> It is futile to try to reconstitute the past from the presents between which it is trapped, either the present which it was or the one in relation to which it is now past. In effect, we are unable to believe that the past is constituted after it has been present, or because a new present appears. If a new present is required for the past to be constituted as past, then the former present would never pass and the new one would never arrive. No present would ever pass were it not past 'at the same time' as it is present; no past would ever be constituted unless it were first constituted 'at the same time' as it was present. This is the first paradox: the contemporaneity of the past with the present that is *was*.
>
> (Deleuze 1994: 81)

For those who are unwilling to count beyond two, or who want to view the world dualistically in terms of subject–object relations, this is an unwanted complication, and yet it is also the only reason that time can be understood, in the way of common sense, as a line of succession: 'Every present passes, in favour of a new present, because the past is contemporaneous with itself as present' (1994: 81). But immediately one accepts that there are two presents, one also has to accept that they continue to multiply. This is the second paradox, which Deleuze calls the paradox of coexistence: 'If each past is contemporaneous with itself, then *all* of the past coexists with the new present in relation to which it is now past' (1994: 81–2). In other words, Deleuze is agreeing with Bergson here that each present present is 'only the entire past in its most contracted state'. These two paradoxes lead to a third, the paradox of pre-existence, according to which 'the pure element of the past in general pre-exists the passing present' (1994: 82). What we have here, then, is an account of cross-contamination of moments on a supposed line of time which endlessly divides a moment between something that it was in itself, something that in itself was a condensation of former moments, and something which is looked back upon from endlessly multiplying positions of retrospect.

The basic consequence for this line of thought is that the past cannot be described neutrally from the present as if the former object were categorically separable from the latter subject. This basic problem is incorporated in the new historicist practices in various ways. In Veeser's well-known list of precepts that characterise the new historicisms, this inseparability of subject and object finds several nuanced expressions:

> New Historicism really does assume: (1) that every expressive act is embedded in a network of material practices; (2) that every act of unmasking, critique and opposition uses tools that it condemns and risks falling prey to the practices it exposes; (3) that literary and non-literary texts circulate inseparably; (4) that no discourse, imaginitive or archival, gives access to the unchanging truth or expresses unalterable human nature; and (5) that a critical method and a language adequate to describe culture under capitalism participate in the economy they describe.
>
> (Veeser 1989: 2)

In different ways every one of these five items describes the impossibility of critical distance, or of separating the present from the past, literature from the world, of the subject from the object of critique and of language from culture. I will return to the question of the separability of literary and non-literary texts below. But for now, the important observation is that this sense of the inseparability of the object and the critique of culture means the past cannot be seen as an unchanging, stable object. On the contrary, most new historicist critiques will view the past as something that can be construed in different ways at different times. This is to say that different construals of the past, whether of a literary text or not, will in some degree constitute a history of the present in that they will construe the past according to contemporary interests, even when they maintain a pretence of neutrality. It is perhaps particularly in British cultural materialism that this potential for the past to be used to generate different meanings according to the interests of the present finds its most complex expressions. The cultural materialist rereadings of Shakespeare (Dollimore and Sinfield 1985; Drakakis 1985), for example, are concerned to divert critical attention away from the idea of Shakespeare's plays as timeless monuments to show how their interpretations differ in terms of their political use, from the sixteenth century to the present day.

It is now possible to bring into focus the idea of historical difference, the idea of uses and interpretations of the past changing over time, and the idea of the inseparability of those different moments. First, we might say that the new historicisms differ from the old in part by virtue of their effort to sustain the difficult philosophical questions about the subject and object of historical knowledge in the practice of historical writing. Second, it can be added that these practices tend to sustain a contradiction between on the one hand the difference between the present and past moments, and on the other hand, the inseparability and therefore unity of the present and the past. Here is Marjorie Levinson's account of the role of difference in historicism's subject–object relations in relation to Romantic studies:

> We want to articulate the literatures of the past in such a way as to accommodate the contingency of the present – the wilfulness of our textual politics – and at the same time, to configurate [sic] that freedom with the particular past that is retextualized. We want a framework that will explain the objective value of a belated criticism, one which reads into the work anticipations that were *not* present in the text's contemporary life, only in its posthumous existence, an existence that turns around and *plants itself* in the past. Within such a framework, today's criticism can assume its properly active, interested 'subject'

role and simultaneously figure as part of the objective field which includes the work: its original political position and its reception history.

Of course, to articulate this framework means giving up our notion of time as something different from histories . . . It means conceiving the epochal distinctiveness of Romantic poetry not, chiefly, as a function of natural and therefore monolithic temporality, but as a result of determinate differences obtaining between the productive formations of the early nineteenth century and the late twentieth century, of the different ideological tasks defined by those formations, and finally, of the diverse kinds or levels of relatedness which those basic differences establish.

(Levinson 1996: 23)

The interest of this passage is that it incorporates three senses of difference which will interact throughout this discussion: the idea of the present as differentiated, the sense of determinate historical differences between the present and the past, and the idea that a different history might be told according to the different interests of a text's reception history. In this *mélange*, the subject and the object are both held together in an inseparable relation, and cleaved apart for their historical differences, like a kind of conceptual suture.

DIFFERENT HISTORIES AND THE POSTMODERN NOVEL

The obvious question to pose here is: how can this kind of complicated philosophical argument be incorporated into the practice of writing history? I think there are many approaches to this question that help to characterise the impact of the concept of difference on the new historicisms in literary criticism. For reasons that will become clear shortly, I would like to begin with an example that does not come from criticism but from the novel. Little argument is required to establish the importance of time in fictional narration. Retrospection is the basis of fiction, so that the novel will always produce some kind of tension between that which is narrated and the voice or position from which it is narrated. For example, in unreliable narration it is common to encounter a narrator whose recall is imperfect, and who makes the reader aware that some invention, some artistic licence is required in the reconstruction of events. This can easily be used for comic and ironic purposes, as for example when Tristram gets stuck in the detail of events prior to his own birth at the beginning of Sterne's *The Life and Opinions of Tristram Shandy* (first published from 1759–67). Similarly the third person narrator/biographer in Woolf's *Orlando* (1928) can declare the complete lack of historical sources for a section of Orlando's life before narrating that period in impossible, and therefore invented, detail. In such cases, fiction is highlighting the artificiality of retrospection, the impossibility of its fidelity to the pastness of the past, or the cross-contamination of the subject as present and the object as past. These are comic examples of a fundamental aspect of fictional narrative, the necessary and yet naturalised component of invention in the act of recall, or the necessity and yet impossibility of third person omniscience in a description of the past.

It may be that the paradoxes of omniscience and unreliable narration are fundamental to narrative, but they also provide the basis for a great deal of contemporary fictional experimentation, and nowhere more so than in the resurgence of the historical novel in the postmodern period. Postmodern fiction is self-consciously preoccupied, in general terms, with questions about the mechanisms of narrative. A postmodern novel will characteristically highlight the normally invisible fictional devices that create the illusion of reference, and in so doing, will conjure a world and at the same time provide a kind of critical commentary on the way in which that world is conjured. For this reason, it is common to find the technical devices or indeed the fundamental presuppositions of the conventional novel actually thematised within a postmodern fiction. This kind of self-commentating, self-analysing, self-referential novel is usually referred to as metafiction, that is, fiction that somehow takes fiction itself as its primary subject. One of the most influential accounts of the nature of postmodern fiction is that of Linda Hutcheon, a contemporary Canadian theorist who claims that it is not merely metafictionality that characterises the postmodern novel, but what she calls historiographical metafictionality (Hutcheon 1988), which is to say that it is the combination of fictional self-consciousness and themes concerned with the knowability of history, that most adequately characterise postmodern fiction.

The notion of historiographical metafiction is a useful encapsulation of the postmodern approach to history because it illustrates two principles underpinning the idea of different histories. The first principle is that history is different from what it used to be because historiographical metafiction is self-consciously aware of the artificiality of retrospect, and of the impossibility of a neutral and objective description of the past. The second principle is that history is different because, as a result of this self-awareness, the historiographical metafiction writes the history of people normally excluded from history, that is, it tells a different story from the official, well-known, well-trodden accounts of the past. In other words, the self-conscious textualism and the liberation of meaning from structures of exclusion that I have described in the previous chapter as characteristics of the new historicisms, taken together with the conviction that the present will always bear the traces of past and future, are exactly the principles that underpin the fictional production of different histories in historiographic metafiction. In fact many have argued that this is not just a question of the novel providing a good medium for the expression of these philosophical and historiographical ideas. Rather the novel is uniquely capable of dealing with the new philosophical uncertainties about the past, uniquely capable of staging the epistemological complexities explored in the philosophy of time, exactly because the novel deals in the texture of lived experience, in the interaction of social and historical forces as they work on individuals. Linda Hutcheon, for example, is one of many critics who thinks that the contemporary relevance of the novel lies exactly in this power to stage philosophical questions about history in a way that traditional discursive philosophy cannot do. 'Postmodern novels', she claims, 'raise a number of issues surrounding the nature of identity and subjectivity; the question of reference and representation; the intertextual nature of the past; and the ideological implications of writing about history' (1988: 117). The new historical novel is highly adapted to these issues exactly because of its heritage of what some have come to call, tautologically, 'self-reflexivity'. Speaking of the American novelist Robert Coover, Hutcheon describes the power of reflexivity in these epistemological terms:

> This self-reflexivity does not weaken, but on the contrary, strengthens and points to the direct level of historical engagement and reference of

the text. Like many postmodern novels, this provisionality and uncertainty (and the wilful and overt construction of meaning too) do not 'cast doubt upon their seriousness', but rather define the new postmodern seriousness that acknowledges the limits and powers of reporting or writing the past, recent or remote.

(1988: 117)

This idea, that fiction, or perhaps literature in general, has an epistemological relevance is by no means new. From Aristotle onwards it is a recurring theme that literature offers access to a more general kind of truth than history precisely by virtue of its ability to balance the universal and particular properties of the objects or events it describes. But what is being said here is a rather more specialised version of that argument, that fiction is especially adapted to the enactment of the uncertainty, or provisionality, that characterises contemporary attitudes to history. For this reason it is also arguable that if fiction has acquired a historiographical importance, the contemporary practice of writing history is just as pre-occupied with historiographical and epistemological questions, and that this preoccupation is reflected in an increased literariness in historical writing. 'The principal faculty involved', says Stephen Greenblatt in his book *Marvelous Possessions*, 'is not reason but imagination' (1988: 17). It is certainly a tendency overwhelmingly in evidence in the New Historicism of the last two decades that imagination has supplanted reason, and that the neutral tones of traditional historicism have yielded to a rampantly tropological language: language pervaded by metaphorical, analogical and associative modes of connection and argumentation. If fiction has been a good medium to raise questions about the uncertainty of historical knowledge, criticism has also deployed what Dominic Lacapra calls the 'paralogical' modes of reasoning normally considered literary to the same ends. Tropological language may then be thought of as an imaginative resource for the writing of history that distinguishes the New Historicisms from 'objective' histories.

LITERARY CANONS AND DIFFERENCE

In his introduction to *The Archaeology of Knowledge* (1972), Michel Foucault outlines his programme for a different kind of historical writing.

Foucault describes the past as a multiplicity of disparate forces in constant battle, which no traditional historical writing can do justice to. The 'historian's history', as he calls it, attempts to trace a continuous line through a disparate past, and in so doing produce an impression that events took place in a causal chain. Against this basic scheme, Foucault formulates an archaeological history that attempts to recover the forgotten areas of human thought, which is to say those huge areas of the past that are suppressed and consigned to oblivion by the historian's history. The linear history is, for Foucault, a structure of exclusion because in the process of constructing the impression of a seamless chain of events, it represses all counter-evidence that would contradict the scheme. This mass of conflicting forces in which events take place, but which are suppressed and excluded by traditional history to create the illusion of a free-standing and continuous sequence, is referred to by Foucault as a 'discursive formation'. I have already argued that the idea of exclusion was, for Foucault, a kind of scaling up of the structuralist account of the sign, and this approach to the sign as a system-bound entity that cannot be taken in isolation can be read in the following account of an event embedded in a discursive formation:

> Is it not possible to make a structural analysis of discourses that would evade the fate of commentary by supposing no remainder, nothing in excess of what has been said, but only the fact of its historical appearance? The facts of discourse would then have to be treated not as autonomous nuclei of multiple significations, but as events and functional segments gradually coming together to form a system. The meaning of a statement would be defined not by the treasure of intentions that it might contain, but by the difference that articulates it upon other real or possible statements, which are contemporary to it or to which it is opposed in the linear series of time.
> (Foucault 1973: xvii)

The principle of difference works for Foucault exactly as it works for the structural linguist except that the repressed context for the historical event is not a system of differences between words but a morass of other events and statements. As for the structuralist sign, the historical event cannot be taken in isolation either from the synchronic formation in which it operates or the temporal sequence of events in which its syntagmatic relations are established.

A very clear example of the functioning of this Foucauldian archaeology can be found in literary history in the idea of the literary canon. One of the major impacts of the New Historicisms in literary studies was the busting of the canon: the demythologisation of literary value, the breaking of male Anglo-Saxon hegemony in literary studies, the destruction of the boundary between high and popular culture. These were campaigns waged by leftist intellectuals against the traditional values of high culture. The enemy in intellectual terms was totalisation: the idea that the history of literature in its entirety could be represented by such a tiny fragment of literature. The literary canon was a *grand narrative* in the sense that it represented the history of literature as a whole as a linear story constructed by sweeping exclusions. With narrative events the size of historical epochs, the canon could only operate in this way, representing national literary history as a sequence of eras, with names like the Renaissance, Romanticism and Modernism, which could be represented in shorthand by a handful of hypercanonised texts. Many of the political problems with the canon were associated with its national character. Within a nation, the canon was understood as a kind of trickle-down economics, where the value and values of great works, as arbitrated by great people with the discrimination to know the good from the bad, functioned as top–down instruction. A kind of narcissism presided over the canon, translating the values of a critical elite into the value of great literature, alleging the universalism of those values. They were values to be adopted by the excluded for edification.

Canon-busting can be understood in Foucauldian terms as a kind of archaeology which sought to displace bogus notions of aesthetic value, or universal human values, and show instead that the very canonicity of a nation's great works is a kind of systematic exclusion of other voices. Just as Foucault talked of uncovering the forgotten areas of human thought in *The Archaeology of Knowledge*, so might literary canon-busting be seen as an attempt to dislodge the apparently metonymic relation between a canonised text and its epoch, by reinstating forgotten texts in the representation of an age. According to the structuralist orientation of Foucault's dream of a systematic account of discourse, the canonicity of a text is structurally dependent on the exclusions that it peforms on others, so that the idea that great works stand on their own and glow in the luminosity of their greatness becomes merely another version of the illusion that words have meaning as free-standing entities. A different history in this case will entail exactly the hidden system of differences, or perhaps power relations, on which the value of a text rests.

There is no doubt that literary history, the canon and the characteristics of literary epochs, which were inherited from mid-twentieth-century literary criticism, have been utterly transformed by criticism of the 1970s onwards. Perhaps most notable in this transformation is the presence of voices excluded from the canon on grounds of gender, race, sexuality and nationality. From this point of view, the creation of a different canon has been a collective project, in the sense that we find the same kind of anti-canonical archaeology taking place in as diverse areas of criticism as queer theory, feminism, postcolonialism and postmodernism.

It is probably apparent that two quite different contexts for the concept of difference are beginning to cooperate in this kind of strategy. The first is the context that has been most discussed so far, that is, the structuralist context of difference, and the structural logic of a system of differences and exclusions at work in discursive formations, whether they are the size of sentences, novels or historical epochs. The second is the context of cultural difference, whereby the domination of one cultural identity by another is opposed in the very act of rewriting history. It was one of Foucault's many achievements to articulate the first context to the second, though some will argue that he grew out of his structuralist ideas in the 1970s and began to focus on questions of power and inequality in more direct ways. However it is interpreted, there is an interesting convergence in Foucault's writing between a structural and a social imperative to embrace difference, which, as I will be going on to discuss, has characterised not only dealings with difference, but contemporary criticism as a whole, ever since.

THE USES OF DIFFERENCE IN HISTORICIST CRITICISM

There is clearly a strong continuity between the structuralist attitude to a linguistic system and Foucault's account of a discursive formation, since neither the sign nor the historical event can be understood except in the context of a larger formation of relations. Structuralism and historicism may have been considered polemical opponents throughout the so-called theory wars of the 1970s and 1980s, but there is something methodologically quite compatible about critical approaches that are, at least at an abstract level, united in their insistence on context, relation and system. If Derrida's reception in North America attests to a high degree of confusion in the factional debate between historicism and formalism, this might act as a more general warning that the ideas of structuralism are by no means simply opposed by historicist criticism. Nor is Foucault alone in having linked structuralist and cultural meanings of difference, and it is possible to find the trace of structuralist ideas in the work of some of the most influential figures of historicist and cultural criticism, such as Clifford Geertz, Pierre Bourdieu and Michel de Certeau. The close relationship between structural linguistics and anthropology in the work of Lévi-Strauss is one path along which structuralist conceptions of difference found their way, via ethnography and sociology, towards historicist modes of criticism. This relationship between linguistic and cultural difference receives more attention in the next chapter. But it might be worth considering for a moment an example of where these two types of difference are not successful accomplices.

In the discussion of Derridean differance, it became clear that far more is at stake than the mere multiplication of histories. It is true that Derrida expressed opposition to notions of a single or general history, and that there was some explicit lobbying for the idea of differentiated and multiple histories. But the concept of differance itself is more bound up with the possibility of a non-metaphysical history, and therefore less with the idea that histories should be many in number than the idea that they should be written in a way that sustains resistance to foundational presences, and the entire system of values that these presences support. It is not enough simply to write more histories. If one does so one has, as the British philosopher David Woods puts it in *The Deconstruction of Time*, 'merely multiplied the heads of the monster, and not slain it, or even tamed it' (1989: 373). Different, pluralised histories may be more democratic, may give voice to the silenced, but do nothing to address what many have taken to be the more pernicious activities of history in reproducing the metaphysical assumptions embedded in the concept of time.

The New Historicisms in literary studies have therefore taken both projects together, and followed the double imperative to write different histories and to write history differently. In the case of the literary critic, who is not primarily a writer of history, this really means writing about literary texts in ways that are historical and yet different from the traditional historicisms of literary studies. I have already analysed the process by which criticism actually becomes more literary, more creative and more aware of the subjectivity of historical perspective. But there were also discernible changes in the way that criticism thought about the historical context of a work of literature, which are often based in Foucault's sense of the connection between the insights of structuralism and questions of politics. In traditional historical criticism, for example, it might have been thought helpful for the critic to research into aspects of historical context that would help shed light on the events and predicaments represented in fiction. Some knowledge of Elizabethen London might be required for the student of Shakespeare, or of the Industrial Revolution to inform the reader of Elizabeth Gaskell.

Foucault's arguments introduced a less obvious version of this kind of historicisation. Rather than representing contextual information that is manifestly relevant to the content of a literary work, Foucault's archaeological perspectives offered the possibility of looking for contextual information which appeared irrelevant, or perversely opposite to that content. There had always been some of this in criticism. It had often been said of Jane Austen, for example, that she left a lot of things out of her novels, the obvious examples being almost everyone beneath the mercantile level of social class and the small issue of the Napoleonic wars. She was, as she declared herself, working on a tiny piece of ivory, and therefore had to exclude almost everything that took place outside a few provincial drawing rooms.

Many of Foucault's followers took the basic idea here, that there might be some systematic exclusion of certain aspects of the world, and applied it much more generally to historical representations. The representation of life in a provincial village, after all, is structurally dependent on the exclusion of something else, so that the full explanation of what it depicts involves the recovery of what it has excluded. This is a basic imperative of much new historicism: that the description of apparently unpolitical things like marriage or the beauty of nature necessarily bear the traces of, say, property and land ownership, but that the political aspects of these subjects are often pushed out, systematically excluded, and become a kind of political unconscious.

This is an exciting idea for literary criticism if only because it opens up so many new possibilities for critical interpretation. In theory there is almost no limit to the political unconscious, or to the historical contexts that literary representations have repressed, just as there is almost no limit to paradigmatic relations that structuralists saw as the unconscious exclusions of language in general. It is nothing less than a licence to write about what is not there in a literary text, to endlessly graft new historical contexts on to literary works and in the process generate endlessly different readings. There are some limitations, for example, for the formalist or the intrinsic critic, to what can be said about Anne's progress towards marriage with Captain Wentworth (*Persuasion*), but for the contextualist for whom what is there depends structurally on what is not, there is a colonial history of Ceylon and an analysis of the sugar trade in the nineteenth century waiting in the margins every time someone in an English village sweetens their tea. Sometimes then the exploration of historical context might seem to be going against the grain of the text under discussion, might seem to be reminding it of repressed historical and political topics or aspects of the world in which it has itself shown no interest. And this is exactly the point of politically motivated historicism of this kind.

One example is the work of Raymond Williams (1921–88), which has inspired an ongoing tradition of cultural materialist criticism in Britain committed to this kind of contextualism. Williams's work on the social history of the countryside, for example, is an extraordinarily patient political debunking of the pastoral mode in literature, its aestheticisation and mythologisation of the past. More recently, Edward Said's work has argued that it is the responsibility of criticism to be *contrapuntal*, a term he borrows from the description of a musical harmony which works against the melody to describe the way that a historical context can be used as a counterpoint to the 'melody' of a literary text. In *Culture and Imperialism* (1994), these contexts are historical perspectives on the global system in which apparently free-standing geopolitical localities – cultural differences – find their structural conditions.

Different histories can therefore also be understood as a range of different interpretations of literary texts, particularly where these contexts seem to work, contrapuntally, against the grain of the texts themselves. But we might also, finally, connect this point, this notion of contrapuntal readings, with the transformation that the new historicisms have brought about in literary canons and therefore in literary history. In the discussion of canon-busting, I said that the reinvention of literary epochs consisted largely in resurrecting and re-evaluating forgotten texts, often by socially marginalised writers, as a kind of political commitment to difference. But this is not the only impact of cultural history on the understanding of literary history. Jameson has argued, for example, that the tendency towards formal fragmentation in the modernist novel cannot be understood in the aesthetic and formalist terms that have dominated the account of the modernist period. Traditionally the fragmentation of the novel is seen either as gratuitous aesthetic experiment or as part of a more general shift in fiction away from the concern to represent external reality towards a concern with interiority and subjective experience. For Jameson, however, the age of empire has turned history into what he calls an 'ungraspable totality' (1990). It is no longer possible to encapsulate society in an English provincial village because society has been transformed into an enormous global complexity, so that what is depicted in an English village is a mere fragment of the whole picture, the ungraspable totality of the global system. The relationship between the bourgeoisie and the proletariat, for example, is no longer observable in a single locality because, in the age of empire, the proletariat is increasingly separated geographically from the bourgeoisie, so that the global picture can be experienced in any one place only in fragments. Individual texts, in other words, present fragments of a much larger picture, which can be brought to bear on their interpretations. The whole assumed character of modernist fragmentation as aesthetic experiment is brought into question by the context of imperialism when an apparently formal aspect of literature is itself historicised. What these arguments point to most directly is the increasing importance of global contexts for a consideration of difference, not only in relation to grand theories of cultural identity, but also in the practices of textual interpretation.

5

CULTURAL DIFFERENCE

We live in a world of difference, a world in which people and places differ from each other. This means that, though there is a complicated philosophical and linguistic background for the term 'difference', there is also a very familiar meaning which describes the diversity of the world. This chapter aims to illustrate that one of the most characteristic and surprising attributes of the term 'difference' is the extent to which it has managed to combine easy, readily understandable meanings with those derived from a more complex theoretical background. As a critical concept, cultural difference often has this doubleness about it: on the one hand the most straightforwardly dull observation that the world is not a singularity, and on the other, the articulation of that observation to a complex theoretical framework.

DIFFERENCE, OTHERNESS AND ALTERITY

If we assume for a moment that difference finds its most modern inspiration in the structuralist movement, it can be recalled that there are two basic assumptions. The first is that language is not merely a nomenclature for entities that exist in the world, but that language has a role in the production of those entities. The second is that the basic unit of meaning for the structuralist is the binary opposition, so that one's sense of the entities existing in the world is a product of the oppositions whose structures we use to interpret reality. This is clearly a way of understanding the structuration of social reality: that a social identity is always embedded in a system of differences, and defined in particular against its opposite. But the word 'opposite' can be misleading.

In chapter 1 of this book, I pointed out that sometimes minor differences seem socially more significant than major ones, according to the logic of Freud's 'narcissism of minor differences'. It certainly seems true of personal identity that one is more likely to abhor people very similar to oneself than those very different, perhaps on the grounds that one's individuality is more threatened by similarity than difference. We might also be tempted to despise in others the qualities that we most fear in ourselves, creating them as our opposite when they are among our closest relations. This confusion, of minor difference with opposition, seems to operate as a structural principle as much in the family unit as in international relations.

One way around the confusion is to substitute the word 'Other' for 'opposite'. Whereas 'opposite' carries with it an implication that an antonymic relation may be rooted in some maximal difference given in nature, 'Other' indicates that the significant relation is not with a natural opposite, but rather the term against which any particular identity consciously or unconsciously defines itself negatively. 'Other' is in fact a natural complement to 'difference'. It has a roughly equivalent weight of baggage from broadly similar traditions. Thus it would be possible to find origins for the notion of the Other in nineteenth-century philosophy, for example in the work of Hegel and Kierkegaard, or certainly in the early twentieth century in Husserl and Heidegger. But as with difference, the concept of otherness can be seen as a matrix of structuralist, psychoanalytic, anthropological and philosophical arguments, the separate theoretical perspectives of which can be impossible to disentangle. The notion of the Other may have some roots in nineteenth-century philosophy, but it is better understood as a structuralist and psychoanalytic name for the inferior member of a hierarchical quasi-opposition. The condition of otherness is not a logical relation as much as a power relation, and for this reason the notion of otherness usually carries with it the entire poststructuralist critique of the structuralist account of opposition, that is, the critique of the innocence of oppositions as outlined in chapter 3. The critique of opposition has two major critical consequences for the analysis of difference, which this chapter aims to illustrate. The first is that the opposition is seen as a basic unit of cultural difference, and the critic's interest lies either in the analysis of the way that opposition works to produce identity, or in the voicing of otherness that is consigned to silence and ineffability, that is to say, actually giving voice to un-represented points of view and identities normally excluded from representation. The second is to liberate the multiplicity of forces and differences that the opposition reduces to a mere dyad: to do away with the opposition and understand difference in more complex and multi-farious ways. These consequences can be illustrated in relation to gender difference, and ideas about the proliferation of differences in relation to the process of globalisation.

SEXUAL DIFFERENCE, OPPOSITION AND ALTERITY

It will be clear from the discussion so far that the history of the concept of difference is very closely bound up with the history of feminism and feminist criticism. Feminism is in fact one of the areas of thought where the theoretical and non-theoretical meanings of difference find their most productive overlaps. Well before the impact of structuralist theory, feminism was debating ideas of sameness and difference as alternative strategies for the pursuit of equality with men. The strategy of sameness would generally entail a conviction of the common humanity between men and women, and pursue equality on the principle that no discrimi-nation should be made between men and women. The strategy of difference, on the other hand, would involve the recognition of women's particularity, usually with reference to the maternal role, and pursue equality through the recognition of this sexual difference. Carol Ann Bacchi, a feminist writer at the University of Adelaide, describes this in *Same Difference* (1990):

> The first clear division of the women's movement into 'sameness' and 'difference' camps occurred in the period between the two world wars. It was the result of the conflict produced when some women rejected their traditional role as 'guardians of the hearth', and sought to engage in free market competition alongside men. Most of these . . . wanted

women to pursue *their* individual self-interest. They spoke in terms of women's 'sameness' to men . . . The majority of those who empha-sised women's *differences* considered traditional sex roles the only means to promote community well-being . . . In the main they did not approve of married women working outside the home and tried to find ways to increase women's economic independence and status within it.

(Bacchi 1990: xiii)

There is clearly no linguistic theory underlying the meanings of same-ness and difference here. These are strategic alternatives based in sexual difference and gender roles. Bacchi goes on to show that these are very limiting positions, and a limited way of understanding the alternatives for the women's movement. There is a danger that, in choosing between the strategies of sameness and difference, no challenge will be issued to the sex-specific characteristics of men, and furthermore, that the whole issue of inequality might be forgotten:

Talking about 'samenesses' and 'differences' also diverts attention from the problem of hierarchy . . . If women are in fact 'different', the question becomes: why has this 'difference' been constructed as disadvantage? If women are in fact the 'same', the problem of their relative disadvantage and lack of power remains unresolved. There is a need therefore to shift the focus of analysis from the 'difference' to the structures which convert this 'difference' into disadvantage.

(Bacchi 1990: xvii)

In the first place then, the term 'difference' in feminist discourse carries this quite straightforward meaning of sexual difference, and of the strategy that asserts that difference in pursuit of equality with men or a critique of patriarchy.

In the 1970s and 1980s, this primary meaning of 'difference' in feminism begins to merge with the more linguistic concept of difference that I have been describing in previous chapters. In an essay published in 1989, Michele Barrett identifies three different meanings of the word 'difference' in recent feminist theory. *Difference I* is what she calls 'straight-forward sexual difference' and corresponds roughly to the dichotomy presented above. *Difference II* is Saussurean difference in which 'meaning is constructed through linguistic opposition rather than through absolute reference' (1989: 41). And *Difference III* is 'effectively a recognition of diversity' (1989: 44). The advantage of the second kind of meaning of 'difference' (*Difference II*) to feminism is that it presents a challenge to what Barrett calls the 'epistemological certainties of much Western social thought' (1989: 41). More specifically, it displaces *essentialism*: the belief that essential and unchangeable characteristics determine social roles, in this case that a woman's social role is underpinned by biology. Much feminist theory takes essentialism as its enemy, and structuralist linguistics (Saussurean difference) offers a theoretical perspective with which to displace an essentialist view of social reality. As it has been argued earlier in this book, a central thesis of structural linguistics is that differences are not given in nature, but constructed by a language that projects its system of differences on to the world. The value of Saussurean difference to feminism therefore is that it can help to displace essentialism and unmask the structuring principles that dupe us into thinking that differences are given in nature.

Earlier, I said that the theoretical and the non-theoretical meanings of 'difference' find their most productive relationship in feminism. Barrett's conclusion about the three different meanings of 'difference' is rather more negative:

> I would want to stress that there are not merely differences between these three deployments of the concept, there are disagreements and outright contradictions. Difference I emphasizes difference between men and women, while Differences II and III emphasize difference 'within' the category of women. Difference II rejects the human subject on which Difference III is predicated. Difference III is also predicated upon the apprehension of an unproblematic ontological reality – the historical and institutional organization of social division – that is explicitly refused by Difference II. Differences I and III incline towards essentialism; Difference II is deconstructive in its approach to gendered subjectivity.
>
> (1989: 46)

Barrett is undoubtedly right here, that the concept of difference in much social theory is a jumble of incompatible meanings. But there are also places, especially where the concept is derived closely from one particular theoretical source, where linguistic theories of difference have enhanced social theories such as feminism.

In France, critics and theorists such as Julia Kristeva, Hélène Cixous and Luce Irigaray can be seen as highly politicised writers who emerge from, and contribute to, the structuralist and poststructuralist accounts of difference. In significantly different ways, Cixous, Kristeva and Irigaray develop an account of the relationship between linguistic and sexual difference that draws on the critique of metaphysical opposition as developed in the work of Derrida, Foucault and Lyotard. Cixous's work, for example, repeatedly returns to the question of opposition as an example of a kind of misfit between words and the world, where the world exists in a more fluid and multiplicitous condition than the rigid terms of linguistic opposition can respect. For Morag Shiach, for example, Cixous's work oscillates between critical and creative, factual and fictional modes because of her 'unease about the capacity of words to hold out against the power of opposition' (1991: 33). But according to Shiach, this produces a dilemma for Cixous:

> She feels the pressure to produce formulae and solutions which are more dogmatic, more rigid, than her understanding of the 'movement' of sexual difference allows. She contemplates the possibility of giving up altogether on the project of trying to talk about sexual difference, about women and the economy of the feminine, since the pressure within this project to reproduce the dominant figures of the 'feminine' is so intense.
>
> (Shiach 1991: 33)

This is a dilemma faced by many of the poststructuralist critics of opposition, namely that the opposition seems to reduce a complex reality to something rigid and confining, and yet, for practical or political reasons it is necessary to continue to use that opposition as a framework for one's thought. Cixous is therefore carrying something of Derrida's strategic adherence to oppositions in the process of deconstruction into the field of sexual difference. Just as Derrida and others have found it necessary to displace the metaphysical oppositions of philosophy through creative, performative and neologistic linguistic strategies of their own, so too

Cixous (as Kristeva would do later) often escapes the strictures of critical discourse for the freedom of drama or poetry.

This reliance on literary langauge produces an interesting variant of what I described, in the previous chapter, as a convergence of literary and theoretical discourse, since for Cixous, this becomes a political imperative. This is how Juliet Flower Macannel describes the alliance of the political and literary:

> Cixous's commitment to the problematic of difference is linked to her more or less absolute commitment to *literary* language. It is a commitment that has clearly shaped her institutional practices . . . It has also shaped her theories of feminine writing (*ecriture feminine*) and shaped her literary criticism into a uniquely poetic prose. It is crucial to note that her procedure as critic, writer and reader is to force sexual difference to the surface of writing – be it theoretical, dramatic, political or poetic in nature – so that the writing at last comes to mirror the schism of language, the internal limit that each 'sex' poses to the other within the 'same' language.
>
> (Macannel 2002: 367)

Two important observations emerge from this link between the political and the literary. The first is that it establishes a firm relationship between the language of a text and the biographical, if not the biological, identity of its author as a kind of context. The second is that it offers the possibility of an account of feminine writing, that is, of a different kind of writing, which she develops extensively throughout her corpus. This idea of the relationship between difference and writing, that it might be possible to define feminine writing not only in relation to the sex of an author, but in qualitative or stylistic terms, has been widely dismissed from both within and outside feminist criticism. But it has also been highly influential for the extent to which it places language, and particularly literary language at the forefront of political debate. This makes Cixous a proponent of the view, which has recurred throughout this discussion, that only by attending to language can one displace the most entrenched assumptions and prejudices about nature and culture, that is, those that reify language, or confuse linguistic with natural reality.

Cixous's writing is one of the places in which theories of linguistic difference can be seen at work in the analysis of cultural difference and lived opposition. In *The Newly Born Woman* (1986), the role of hierarchical opposition in thought is clearly identified with male power:

> We see that 'victory' always comes down to the same thing: things get hierarchical. Organization by hierarchy makes all conceptual organization subject to man. Male privilege, shown in the opposition between *activity* and *passivity*, which he uses to sustain himself. Traditionally, the question of sexual difference is treated by coupling it with the opposition, activity/passivity.
>
> (Cixous and Clement 1986: 64)

Many of the difficulties of Cixous's work, from the point of view of her critics, revolve around the undefined but much relied upon category of 'woman', which has been viewed within French feminism as a kind of betrayal of political projects that downplay or deny the importance of sexual difference, or that seek a genuine escape from the binary opposition man/woman. It is probably fair to say that Cixous's use of 'difference' is at times theoretically quite thin, and therefore most in danger of simply collapsing into the most commonplace and literal meanings of the word 'difference'.

A more substantial theoretical elaboration of difference for feminism can be found in the work of Luce Irigaray, whose career provides a strong set of continuities from the early structuralist meaning of the term. Irigaray is particularly influenced by the Derridean critique of difference, its corrective emphasis on temporality, and the account of linguistic opposition as rooted in hierarchy. But whereas Derrida gives the impression of being primarily concerned with metaphysical roots for ethical and political issues, Irigaray's thought, especially in her later career, is closely influenced by the writings of Emmanuel Levinas (1906–99), a French philosopher whose work centres on the attempt to describe ethical responsibility through the idea of otherness. Levinas's thought is important for the philosophy of difference because it establishes the face-to-face encounter with 'the Other' as the site of ethical responsibility. The sense of otherness that we find in structuralism, in which the other is a kind of unconscious, unacknowledged opposite, therefore finds an ethical and political dimension in Levinas's thought. This continuity, from structuralism to poststructuralism and a Levinasian ethics might be simply represented in the following summary. According to the structuralist account of difference, the identity of something always resides in part somewhere else, and perhaps most obviously in its negative or opposite. An identity is never complete in itself, and therefore any exploration that seeks to define an identity will falter, for two reasons. The first is that it will encounter a constituent element of the Other in that identity, and the second is that the identity will also belong to a group, such as a gender. But this alterity (or otherness) in an identity is also a kind of power relation, in that its apprehension is appropriative, in so far as it will seek to dominate and absorb the otherness against which it is defined. When Irigaray talks of a 'disappropriative' relation to the Other, she is therefore invoking this relational model of the subject, in which identities are incomplete, and adding to it a deconstructive strategy in which an identity is partly constituted by a negative, and in which the Other is not to be dominated but respected, as if it were part of oneself. It is common in recent feminist theory in the United States to hear this emphasis described as a move away from the notion of a *difference between* towards a *difference within*.

Much of Irigaray's theory is based on the ethical philosophy of Levinas, the basic commitment of which was that an ethical act involves the respect of alterity or otherness. But the emphasis on sexual difference offers a set of further possibilities, which give Irigaray's work an interesting influence on accounts of culture at large. It is implicit in the summary above that a gender is one of those identity positions which is inhabited by alterity, and therefore that its exploration entails an ethical respect for the negative, or opposite term that partly constitutes it. But Irigaray also makes this claim the other way around. In several of her later works, in which the Levinasian influence is most apparent, she makes the claim that sexual difference is something like a fundamental parameter of the socio-cultural order, and not only that, but a universal condition. She argues that, as a result of this cultural centrality, the culture of sexual difference has a special relevance for other issues of cultural difference, indeed for all cultural difference: that sexual difference is a kind of training for the ethical respect for alterity of all kinds, and that it therefore fosters ethical action conceived, in Kristeva's phrase, as a negativizing of narcissism. If this idea, that sexual difference fosters ethical action by rehearsing respect for otherness, seems vague, it is probably because Irigaray never gives it any exact formulation. Nowhere is this more clear than in *An Ethics of Sexual Difference* (1993), where she makes much of the idea that sexual difference does not yet exist, except as some notional future possibility. If sexual difference does not yet exist, in the sense that it has not yet been apprehended according to this logic of negativity and disappropriation, Irigaray's ethical scheme reproduces another important dimension of Levinas's ethics. Levinas has a similar sense that the responsibility towards the Other encounters grave difficulties, which can be met only by striving towards forms of contact with the Other that have not yet come into focus from the future. Yet without the mystery that such vagueness borrows from the future, there is a feeling that the entire theoretical apparatus of ethical respect amounts to little more than the edict that one should do as one would be done by.

The powerful thing about Irigaray's work, then, is its ability to link ideas of difference, especially as they are developed in French post-structuralism, with questions in cultural politics. Here again, we see the strength and the weakness of the coexistence of difficult theoretical and easy commonplace meanings of the word 'difference'. On the one hand the career of the term 'difference' seems to furnish political and cultural theory with a sophisticated theoretical tradition, and on the other its ethical insights can seem to amount to very little, in terms of a concrete programme for action, in the eyes of the world. This is an accusation that has been levelled repeatedly at Jean-François Lyotard's concept of the *differend*, which similarly attempts to elaborate an ethics based on poststructuralist approaches to difference. Yet Lyotard remains most convincing when the meaning of difference is at its most mundane, and least convincing when it draws suggestively on its many theoretical contexts.

THE DIFFEREND

When cultural critics from different theoretical standpoints talk of alterity, it usually means more or less the same thing: the general property of otherness as the secondary identity in relation to which a dominant identity is structured. But there is another important aspect of alterity and otherness, which is important to identify for the discussion of cultural difference. Alterity often refers to a kind of other-worldliness, to an ungraspable or ineffable quality of the Other. This is particularly evident in postcolonial studies, where racial otherness is often understood as exactly this incomprehensibility and hence unrepresentability of the native by a western coloniser, tourist or writer. The notion of the ineffability of the Other can also be found in the work of Levinas and his many disciples, who have taken the idea of alterity not as an issue concerned with the structuring of identity, but as a site of exchange or encounter with another person, and therefore as the basis of ethical action. It is worth remembering that the concept of the Other has three important characteristics, which find expression in these very different contexts: the sense of quasi-oppositionality, the sense of implicit inferiority or secondariness, and the sense of unknowability or ineffability. These characteristics are in effect accounts of identity as a kind of relation or exchange with the Other, and have been widely used to describe cultural interaction either, with Levinas, on a model of face-to-face interpersonal relations, or, in a more psychoanalytic context, as an unconsious symbolic relation with an opposite or quasi-opposite. From this combination of structuralist, psychoanalytic and philosophical issues it is possible to sketch an ethical and political set of meanings for the concept of difference, and one of the most direct ways of doing so is through an examination of Lyotard's term 'differend'. Lyotard begins his work *The Differend* with the following account:

> As distinguished from a litigation, a differend would be a case of conflict, between (at least two) parties, that cannot be equitably resolved for the lack of a rule of judgement applicable to both arguments. One side's legitimacy does not imply the other's lack of legitimacy. However, applying a single rule of judgement to both in order to settle their differend as though it were merely a litigation would wrong (at least) one of them (and both of them if neither side admits the rule).
>
> (1988: xi)

A differend therefore is an actual and unsolvable dispute which is in a sense generated by unbridgeable cultural difference. The impossibility of legislation in the event of a differend is the result of there being no shared values on which the conflict might be resolved, so that the differend is exactly the name of the unsolvability of a dispute across cultural difference. One of the interesting things about this use of, or adaptation of the term 'difference' is that it draws together some very different strands of the discussion of difference so far. The first of these is the idea dealt with in chapter 1 and chapter 2, that the structuralist concept of difference involved a suspension, if not a critique, of the idea of linguistic reference. Lyotard's account of the incommensurability of different social groups and the unsolvability of conflicts is expressed throughout *The Differend* in very metalingual terms, which is to say that social and political conflicts are described throughout as if they were problems in discourse. In truth, Lyotard's style is a strange mix of legalese (of plaintiffs and victims, juries and litigation) and the vocabulary of the linguist (of phrases and discourses, genre and grammar). The salient idea from structuralism at work here is that there can be no appeal to a sub-linguistic reality as the basis for litigation in a dispute, so that actual conflicts in the world are often cast in this way:

> Reality is not what is 'given' to this or that 'subject', it is a state of the referent (that about which one speaks) which results from the effectuation of established procedures defined by a unanimously agreed upon protocol, and from the possibility offered to anyone to recommence this effectuation as often as he wants.
>
> (Lyotard 1988: 4)

It is probably clear that Lyotard's ethics emerge from a discursive account of political reality which shares something of Edward Sapir's sense of social reality, being determined in language, and therefore something of Foucault's discursive view of history. As I argued in chapter 1, Lyotard is also one of those philosophical thinkers who find the roots of a political philosophy of difference much more obviously articulated in Kant and Hegel than in Saussure and his structuralist followers. Whereas the philosophy of Kant and Hegel represents for Lyotard the possibility of truth and justice as the outcome of philosophical inquiry, Lyotard turns to Wittgenstein, and his vision of a multiplicity of language games for a less teleological, and indeed less hopeful, account of the dynamics of difference. Christopher Norris describes this project, in *The Oxford Companion to Philosophy*, as 'a *mélange* of Wittgensteinian, poststructuralist and kindred ideas presented in an oracular style that raises bafflement to a high point of principle' (1995). Although this is quite adequate as a summary of Lyotardian ethics, it is worth dwelling a little on the idea of bafflement as a high point of principle. It was observed a moment ago that alterity carried among its many meanings that of un-representability or ineffability, and we can observe the importance of this kind of otherness to Lyotard's account of the differend throughout his discussion:

> The differend is the unstable state and instant of language wherein something which must be able to be put into phrases cannot yet be. This state includes silence, which is a negative phrase, but it also calls upon phrases which are in principle possible. This state is signalled by what one ordinarily calls a feeling: 'One cannot find words', etc. A lot of searching must be done to find new rules for forming and linking phrases that are able to express the differend disclosed by the feeling, unless one wants this differend to be smothered right away in a litigation and for the alarm sounded by the feeling to have been useless. What is at stake in a literature, in a philosophy, in a politics perhaps, is to bear witness to differends by finding idioms for them.
>
> (1988: 13)

What he seems to be arguing here is that the differend, in addition to being an irresolvable conflict, is also the not yet sayable, the so far ineffable, and that it is the project of literature, philosophy and politics no less, to try to bring it into the domain of representation. This is an argument with a strong tradition and prehistory in the twentieth century. In modernist literature, for example, there is a recurrent interest in things that are inexpressible, things that language cannot express, areas of experience to which linguistic expression is simply inadequate. This is often referred to as a 'crisis in language', and is particularly associated with modernism's interest in the relatively unchartered, interior and subjective experiences of the human mind. The emphasis placed on unsayability, inexpressibility and ineffability in Lyotard might therefore be seen as a kind of modernist crisis of language finding its way through Barthes and others into philosophy, and therefore back into literary criticism.

Derrida's account of logocentrism, which argues that the metaphysics of presence is somehow in-built in language, gives the idea of neologism a new authority in much poststructuralism, and as I have mentioned, Levinas adds an ethical dimension to the ineffability of the Other. Lyotard's understanding of this seems to draw simultaneously on something like the critique of foundations that we have followed in Derrida's account of differance, but there is clearly also something disappointingly familiar about the core idea: feelings which escape words. In this sense, the differend might be seen as an example of the uneasy relationship between the theoretical and the familiar that inhabits the concept of difference in general.

Where Lyotard's writing is more helpful in relation to difference is in the better-known material addressed to the question of postmodernity. *The Postmodern Condition* is similarly influenced by the Wittgensteinian notion of language games and a poststructuralist emphasis on the discursivity of social life, but it also provides a sociological account of a certain kind of loss, namely the loss of belief in metanarratives. As Lyotard describes it, this loss is primarily the breakdown of belief in the idea of history as progress, whether it be scientific progress, the progress of metaphysics towards truth or the progression towards salvation and justice that he sees in Marx. These grand narratives, as he describes them, have splintered in the postmodern age into *petits recits*, or smaller, more localised stories less concerned with the grand sweep of history or the possibility of universal truth. The splintering described by Lyotard is therefore also a loss of unity, and a loss of the very possibility of consensus. Here for example is the short version of Lyotard's objection to the work of Jürgen Habermas, the leading Frankfurt School social critic, and his rather optimistic emphasis on the possibilities of communication and consensus:

> Is legitimacy to be found in consensus obtained through discussion, as Jürgen Habermas thinks? Such consensus does violence to the heterogeneity of language games. And invention is always born of dissention. Postmodern knowledge is not simply a tool of the authorities; it refines our sensitivity to differences and reinforces our ability to tolerate the incommensurable.
>
> (Lyotard 1983: 5)

It is a widely held view of the contemporary world that it is characterised by proliferating differences and perhaps therefore by an increased sensitivity to difference and toleration of otherness. Whether this view is defensible or not, Lyotard does certainly appear to be right that communication cannot simply be viewed as a means to generate consensus, and that it might be more accurate to say that communication actually generates incommensurability in the act of bringing differences into contact with each other.

FRAGMENTATION, POSTMODERNITY AND COMMERCE

If we look away, for a moment, from the disciplines of literary studies and philosophy, towards sociology, cultural geography and media studies, it is easy to find these complex relations of cultural unity and difference at work. Many cultural geographers and theorists have taken as a fundamental precept of postmodernity the idea that increased communication might actually generate difference. The process of globalisation is usually understood, in this light, as a paradox. Globalisation is, at one level a process of unification, of coming together, of increased communication as described, for example, by Appadurai (1996). It is common also to find commentators describing postmodernity as a condition of fragmentation, of splintering, and as a process of devolution into ever smaller and more local identities. The emphasis on small units, particularities and locality in globalisation can be found equally in academic contexts, as the discussion of literary canons in the previous chapter illustrates, and in the corporate world of business. There is, for example, a move away from the Fordist values of mass production and economies of scale towards what has recently been called 'downsizing', that is, the contraction of the scale of production, and diversification, which is often conceived as a particularisation of production. This is fundamentally a view of globalisation *as* proliferation of difference, and it provides a basis for the difference between modernity and postmodernity that differs from dominant sociological accounts. Sociology has until recently understood the process of globalisation as standardisation. Many cultural critics have argued that this is above all a process of Americanisation, where the political and economic dominance of the United States is felt across the globe. Americanisation was a particularly modernist idea, in the sense that it was seen in terms of a grand narrative progressing towards global homogeneity perceived as modernisation and perfectibility. But in the age of space-time compression, as David Harvey names the contraction of the world (1989), globalisation is no longer understood as a linear narrative of progress towards homogenisation, so that postmodernity is often characterised in Lyotardian terms as the conquest of difference over standardisation:

> If one of the characteristics associated with postmodernism is the loss of a sense of common historical past and the flattening and spatialization out of long established symbolic hierarchies, then the process of globalization, the emergence of the sense that the world is a single place, may have directly contributed to this perspective through bringing about a greater interchange and clashing of different images of global order and historical narratives. The perception of history as an unending linear process of the unification of the world with Europe at the centre in the nineteenth century and the United States at the centre in the twentieth century, has become harder to sustain with the beginnings of a shift in the global balance of power away from the West.
>
> (Featherstone 1993: 171)

Featherstone seems to acknowledge here that the fragmentary character of postmodernity may be no more than a transition from one form of domination to another. Some have seen the process as no more than the diversification of capital, where the process of standardisation masquerades as diversity by commodifying all cultural difference.

The importance of this kind of argument is that it presents a challenge to the view that postmodernity is simply a cultural condition characterised by fragmentation and difference with the contention that it is a two-sided condition in which fragmentation and difference are actually produced by opposite processes of unification and standardisation. If it is a received view that modernity is somehow characterised by the Fordist values of standardisation, and postmodernity by the values of difference, the dialectical view offers an account in which the forces of standardisation and diversification actually coexist in the contemporary world, as if modernity and postmodernity exist in a necessary relationship. There are some well-known buzz words in media and cultural studies and in marketing, whose function seems to be, above all, to imply the victory of difference. The idea of *niche marketing* is an example from the 1980s of a perceived shift away from the *catch-all* advertising campaigns of previous decades. Niche marketing can be understood in two ways: either as the increasingly focused targeting of a marketing strategy towards a narrow sector of the population, or as the increasingly specialised function of retail outlets. In either case, there seems to be a logic of difference, of responding to and generating difference in the market, at work in the service of commercial aims. We might view in the same light the shift away from the outright commitment to standardisation at work in a corporation such as McDonalds, whose early global adventures were predicated on the absolute standardisation of food menus, and who have since yielded to the diversification of menus as a gesture towards the mounting protest against its disregard of cultural difference.

In media studies, the analogous transition is the shift from broadcasting to *narrowcasting*, in which national television and radio events of the 1960s and 1970s with audiences larger than any now attained, have been fragmented by the proliferation of specialised television channels and programmes. But narrowcasting, like the diversification of McDonalds's menus and niche retail outlets on the High Street, is something of a sham in the sense that the fragmentation of broadcasting seems to be simply a commercial strategy; it produces difference in order to renew and expand markets that were once flattened by the aspirations towards universality implicit in broadcasting. It is clear that broadcasting is not only still with us, but that its scale has expanded from a national to a global arena. It is difficult to argue that narrowcasting is a defining characteristic of the contemporary media world and at the same time heed the rise of CNN or the expansion of Time Warner in the entertainment sector. In these contexts, difference is a straightforward commercial principle which seeks to disguise the global domination of corporate capital as individuality and difference.

Given the individualist and commercial logic of difference in the marketplace, it is unsurprising to find that the leftist view of cultural difference comes under considerable ideological stress, particularly where political-governmental and commercial meanings of standardisation and unification collude. The Conservative government in Britain in the 1980s, for example, viewed the idea of the unification of Europe as a threat to the individuality and freedom of the nation state. The dichotomies of large and small seemed to be under ideological stress in this period because devolution into ever-decreasing units of identity seemed to defend the political right wing, its traditional nationalist stance, its emphasis on individuality, and the idea of sovereignty. Society was seen as a socialist or even Soviet concept, a concept without a referent in the then Prime Minister Margaret Thatcher's much quoted view. Yet the European Community, especially as it was conceived in the 1980s, was nothing more than an enormous free trade zone, a capitalist monolith underwritten by the values of the free flow of capital. Nobody would expect the poles of large and small to correspond in any way to political positions, but there is sometimes a surprising slippage in cultural theoretical argument, no less than in party politics, between the large and small and the political left and right. It is common, for example, to find ideas of difference and particularity, region and locality, invoked in the name of a leftism that the left does not support per se. This tension between difference as a counter-politics and difference as a commercially based individualism might also be bound up with the problem at the very heart of the critical concept of difference. I have argued that the structuralist and poststructuralist conceptions of difference were always courted by an ambiguity, a mutual contamination between subject and object. The clearest illustration of this ambiguity has been the structuralist uncertainty about whether linguistic differences are properties of the world subsequently registered in the language system, or differences projected on to the world by that system. According to the first view, differences are discovered by language, and according to the second, they are invented by language. The same might be said of differences in the two domains of production and consumption in the marketplace. The consumer is inclined to believe that the proliferation of different products in the supermarket, High Street or on television reflects the rich diversity of individual customers. But to view differences between customers as pre-existing and objective is to deny, and yield to, the active invention of those differences by the ongoing process of product differentiation. One of the dangers of the coexistence of complex critical meanings and familiar meanings in the word 'difference' is exactly this danger of the slippage between the bourgeois individualism of the consumer and the pedigree of difference as a form of ideological critique, as the widespread use of Deleuze and Guattari's ideas by advertising agencies confirms.

6

DIFFERENCE AND EQUIVALENCE

In chapter 1 and chapter 2 it was apparent that the structuralist concept of difference contained a paradox. It may be that the founding insight of structural linguistics was that meaning was generated by difference between words, but there was also a sense in which difference was effaced by structuralist analysis. The structuralist anthropologist was intent on finding equivalence between different kinship systems, different wedding ceremonies and different myths. Similarly, the structuralist literary critic would establish a kind of equivalence between literary texts, finding deep structures in literary narratives that would represent a common denominator in them, and in the process dissolving their individuality into a kind of abstract algebra. This phenomenon was a function of the scientific emphasis of the structuralist project. When we follow the progress of difference through the poststructuralist notion of irreducible difference and into the various formulations of cultural difference in social theory, we find a more genuinely individuating species of analysis emerging, in which the particularity, historical specificity and unique texture of a literary work, an identity or a culture finds its place. And yet it should also be apparent that the pole of equivalence has never quite disappeared in this discussion. The deconstructive reading, for example, is often focused on the resistance an individual text puts up to a model of analysis that seeks to assimilate it to others, and yet deconstructive readings have also been accused of generating the same object repeatedly: of producing literary texts repeatedly as allegories of the elusiveness of meaning. In the discussion of postmodernity and globalisation it was clear that cultural difference is particularly in evidence when it exists alongside cutural standardisation, or even that difference is generated by sameness in cultural terms, as a defensive strategy. Even the New Historicisms and postcolonial criticisms have had their fair share of the accusation that they produce similarity or homogeneity among their objects of analysis. It would appear, then, that the pole of equivalence continues to haunt the concept of difference no matter how much that concept seeks privilege or autonomy. In more recent years, at the end of the twentieth century and at the start of the next, there has been a more concerted move, a distinguishable trend to recover the idea of equivalence. There has been a feeling, particularly in left political thought, that we have dwelled for too long on questions of difference, or that we have become over-Lyotardian in our belief that cultures are somehow incommensurable, incapable of communication, negotiation, or common ground. Since the mid-1990s it is possible to trace a pronounced shift in the other direction, in an attempt to emphasise not difference but similarity, equivalence, even to retrieve the notion of universality.

The idea of universality is, once again, one of the thorny questions of philosophy in the analytical and Continental traditions. Universality has also been one of the most celebrated casualties of the epoch of difference, in that the continuous honing of the concept of difference in the twentieth century was also a process of refining the critique of traditional accounts of universality. Lyotard's declaration of the end of grand narratives is one example, and the notion of the differend is a direct declaration of the death of anything that might be considered as a universal value. But it may be the gross exaggeration at the heart of postmodern theory, the exaggeration that claims the triumph of difference at the expense of universality that has been responsible for this resurgence. It is as if we have lived through a period of repression, in which the pole of equivalence lurks in the unconscious of our most favoured concepts, and the values of universality have continued, unacknowledged, to inhabit the logic of our rampant particularism. In this chapter we shall explore a contemporary debate about the refurbishment of the universal, and look at two formulations of the new universal as they relate to the concept of difference.

CONCRETE UNIVERSALITY AND METAPHOR

It has been argued at various points in this discussion that the concept of difference overlaps significantly with the values of particularism. It is important, however, to distinguish two closely related types of particularism as they are to be found in literary studies. The first is an identity particularism, whereby the largest totalities such as humankind, or epochal totalities such as romanticism or modernism, are dismantled to reveal a multitude of previously effaced differences of race, class, and gender. The second is a particularism of method motivated by historical specificity, whereby the literary critic focuses attention on increasingly small units of cultural meaning, such as objects or events that carry within them an explanation of something much larger than themselves. In criticism, this second type of particularism is evident in the demise of grand critical projects. One no longer goes to conferences to hear papers about speech-act theories of literary discourse, or principles of unity in *Ulysses*. There is a move towards explorations of the cultural metaphoricity of atomic details, such as the history of the typewriter, telegraphy and telepathy, the cigarette in modernism, late nineteenth-century refuse collection, the gas lamp in Victorian London, skin as a cultural metaphor, or rats in literature.

The climate of particularism in criticism is also deeply bound up with the demise of literary theory. During its period of greatest influence, literary theory functioned in criticism as a kind of court of arbitration in which the methods and truth claims of criticism sought the basis of their validity. If literary theory was a place for the evaluation of truth claims, the formulation of general laws and the sponsorship of linguistic science, this kind of particularism flourished precisely through its opposition to these pretensions. In the cultural historical writings of literary critics, for example, particularism meant a complete departure from the abstractions of theory, and an anchorage of criticism in the material specificities of cultural context. And yet, as I have already suggested, this particularism was never as thoroughgoing as it might be exactly because the atomic cultural detail seized upon by the cultural historical critic is never merely something in itself, something entirely concrete or material. Almost invariably, the meaning of a detail in this kind of new historicism is displaced, or projected outwards to the more general claims that might have once been ventured by theoretical discourse, but that now find expression only in implicit and metaphorical modes.

Metaphor is, after all, the trope of similarity, the trope of equivalence, a kind of crossing point between the logic of difference and the logic of equivalence. A metaphor is both something in itself, and a relation to something else, a thing and a similarity. When literary critics, for example, turn their hand to the cultural history of ventriloquy, or telegraphy, as they have done, there is a clear sense that these are theoretical metaphors, capable of evoking an elaborate thematics about voice, communication, distance and responsibility. When a literary critic specialises in Victorian sewage systems it is commonly a part of a larger interest in the imagery of water, of purity and contamination, and therefore with a kind of cultural history that can be told through the story of metaphors. The most prominent of the American New Historicists such as Stephen Greenblatt are prone to find in some small detail a microcosm of the functioning of state power. In other words, in each case, a particularity is not really a particularity at all, but a detail capable, metaphorically or metonymically, of resonating a theoretical and a universal significance. This kind of criticism is both particularist (apparently committed to the irreducible difference of its objects), and universalist (committed to the general economy in which these details circulate), at the same time. These universalising habits of mind may be particularly well-developed in the new literary historicisms because literary critics are particularly aware of, and expert in the interpretation of, metaphor. History provides a forum for the demonstration of skills in the metaphorical, analogical and allegorical interpretation of details. In this kind of critical writing, miscellaneous cultural fragments will often aggregate into collectives or turn outwards towards portentous universals.

These aspects of the New Historicisms have not passed unnoticed. The American deconstructionist critic Hillis Miller, for example, sees the particularism of contemporary criticism as a problem that he refers to as 'biological synecdoche', a kind of argument in which a small detail is seen to bear within it the pattern of a complex whole, through a relation of apparently biological necessity. Similarly Dominic La Capra cautions against what he calls world-in-a-grain-of-sand arguments in the New Historicisms, and their incumbent paralogical methods implying universals by analogy and association, and complains that the value of logic in critical argument is being steadily replaced by the importance of being interesting. The objection to biological synecdoche, or the world in a grain of sand, is partly then an objection to a new logical slipperiness, by which complex totalities once deemed unrepresentable or ungraspable by speculative reason, are rehypothesised in a mode of nervous insinuation; they can then retreat to the alibis of particularity and historical specificity if that hypothesis is questioned. These new particulars are, in short, metaphors masquerading as microcosms.

What is being said here is that the particulars of criticism are capable of being universal at the same time, and so of doing the work once performed by literary theory. But if metaphor is the suggestive mode of this particularist universality, it looks as if criticism is imitating the strategies of literature. If contemporary criticism is characterised by an unusual degree of particularity combined with an unusual ability to imply universality, if metaphor and synecdoche are the means by which criticism can project the meaning of details beyond their particularity, it begins to look as if criticism is the reprise of its own critical object. It is, after all, about the most persistent critical view from Aristotle onwards, that literature is distinguished from history and philosophy on the basis of its equilibrium between particular and universal significance. The pioneering American New Critic William Wimsatt argues this in *The Verbal Icon*:

> whether or not one believes in universals, one may see the persistence in literary criticism of a theory that poetry presents the concrete and the universal, or the individual and the universal, or an object which in a mysterious and special way is both highly general and highly particular.
>
> (1970: 72)

Wimsatt is following several early twentieth-century New Critics, particularly John Crowe Ransom and Allen Tate, in borrowing from Hegel's account of the work of art as a kind of concrete universal:

> In comparison with the show or semblance of immediate sensuous existence or of historical narrative, the artistic semblance has the

> advantage that in itself it points beyond self, and refers us away from itself to something spiritual which it is meant to bring before the mind's eye . . . The hard rind of nature and the common world give the mind more trouble in breaking through to the idea than do the products of art.

> (Wimsatt 1970: 72)

This idea, that art and poetry can show objects that point beyond themselves, was highly influential in the nineteenth century, and underlay much of the writing of English Romantic poets. Similarly, the philosopher, critic and writer John Ruskin (1819–1900), well known for his God-in-a-blade-of-grass arguments, thought that natural objects might have the structure of the concrete universal on their own account, remarking in *Modern Painters* that poetry is not distinguished from history either by the omission or addition of details: 'There must be something either in the nature of the details themselves, or the method of using them, which invests them with poetical power.' It is this ambiguity, I think, between whether particular details are containers of an extended significance in themselves, or have that significance invested in them by the possessor of poetical power, that animates the new particularisms of contemporary literary criticism. If a metaphor is a figure constitutively split between its particularity and its equivalence to something else, it is the trope allowing the new cultural historicisms simultaneously to apprehend the past as past, in its particularity, and to signify beyond itself to something that transcends that particularity, such as the present.

It may be that new particularisms have something in common with poetic power conceived as the concrete universal, and it is certainly common to find the new cultural historians themselves establishing this link between creativity and criticism. One example is Terry Eagleton describing Walter Benjamin's style of microscopic sociology:

> In this kind of microanalysis, the individual phenomenon is grasped in all of its overdetermined complexity as a kind of cryptic code or riddling rebus to be deciphered, a drastically abbreviated image of social processes which the discerning eye will persuade it to yield up.

> (1990: 329)

'What this method then delivers', he says a little later 'is a kind of poetic or novelistic sociology in which the whole seems to consist of nothing but a dense tessellation of graphic images; and to this extent it represents an aestheticised model of social enquiry' (1990: 329–30). Eagleton also explicitly links this with James Joyce's use of myth in *Ulysses*, which he describes as a return of the Romantic symbol, a reinvention of the Hegelian 'concrete universal' in which 'every phenomenon is secretly inscribed by a universal law, and any time, place or identity pregnant with the burden of the cosmic whole' (1990: 319).

What is most striking about this view of criticism as on the one hand a kind of micro-analysis and on the other a kind of novelistic sociology, is that it draws together two major themes of this discussion. In chapters 2–4 the relationship between literature and criticism was described in various ways in terms of a cross-contamination, from the historiographical role of the novel to the creative and inventive properties of criticism and history. It is undeniable that we have recently lived through an age in which literature and criticism have been on convergent paths. On the side of criticism, aestheticisation has been underpinned by a set of theoretical positions that declares that a critic does not describe a literary text objectively, or from a position of neutrality, but rather creates it, invents it, or performs it. Fundamentally this view is based in a constitutive account of language: that language does not describe or reflect reality, it constitutes reality. A much favoured terminology is that language is performative, not constative, in that it brings a state of affairs into existence rather than describes a state of affairs in a way that could be adjudged true or false. It is from this point of view that Barthes can declare that there are no more critics, only writers, in other words no neutral descriptions of literary objects, but only creative inventions of them. On the other side of the boundary, the corollary of aestheticised criticism is literature which is increasingly critical or theoretical, in the sense that it assimilates and incorporates critical and theoretical perspectives into its discourse as self-knowledge. The most obvious example of this is metafiction, self-conscious fiction that reflects critically upon itself or on the nature of novels in general, that is, self-referential, self-knowing fiction, or critical fiction. But it is now possible to link this general picture of creative criticism and critical literature to the dialectical logic of sameness and difference, particularism and universalism, described in chapters 4 and 5.

PARTICULARISM AND GLOBALISATION

We have already suggested that particularism in criticism might be thought of first as a replication of the microscopic sciences, and second as a replication of the concrete universality of literature. We must now consider a third possibility, that the increasing interpenetration of particulars and universals might reflect, or be produced by, the process of globalisation, so that the concrete universal might actually be seen to belong to the cultural logic of standardisation and difference discussed in the previous chapter. Recent social theory of globalisation has a complex tropology that imagines the world as an increasingly small place, a global village, a tiny unity by comparison with the vast complexity that it used to be. One version of this argument is what David Harvey calls 'time-space compression': the idea that as travel speeds have increased from the horse to jet aviation, the world has contracted. Similarly the imagery describing telecommunications and the internet is often that of the increased singularity and visibility of the globe. The largest totality therefore becomes more visible, both because the world can be seen as a single place, a small particularity (the view of earth from outer space), and because trade and tourism produce microcosms of the earth as a whole, exemplified in the supermarket, or Disney World, as sites of the semiotic consumption of cultural difference. However, as the previous chapter argues, the kink in this view is that the social theory of globalisation has shifted in recent decades away from the traditional understanding of globalisation as standardisation. If globalisation is, as many have argued, primarily a process of Americanisation, this standardisation entails a loss of cultural diversity as American cultural forms and influences spread across the world. According to this view, globalisation threatens cultural difference, threatens to homogenise diversity in the name of modernisation. It is when cultural theory recognises that cultural difference is not in retreat, that in fact the process of globalisation might actually generate difference, that the threat of standardisation comes to be seen as the source of a counter-politics of the local. Most cultural theorists since Heidegger have recognised that if globalisation is conceived as a process of compression and unification, it is at the same time a process of diversification, of an increasing awareness of diversity or an increasing individuation of cultures on the global stage. There is an idea that resistance is local, and corporate capitalism is global. The dichotomy of the universal and the particular, the cosmopolitan and the parochial, is therefore sometimes thought of as a dichotomy of power and its resistance. The proliferation of difference and the standardisation of the world seem to go hand in hand, so that globalisation is both convergence and dissemination. What this necessitates, then, is an account of the interpenetration of the universal and the particular that finds its philosophical expression in Hegel and Heidegger and its political reality in the complicity of homogenisation and diversification.

The sociologist Roland Robertson, for example, describes recent history as follows:

> In recent world history, the universalism–particularism issue has come to constitute something like a global-cultural form, a major axis of the structuration of the world as a whole. Rather than simply viewing the theme of universalism as having to do with principles that can and should be applied to all, and that of particularism as referring to that which can and should be applied only locally, I suggest that the two have become tied together as part of a globewide nexus.
>
> (1992: 102)

As if in homage to what Harvey calls 'the increasing interpenetration of opposite tendencies in capitalism as a whole' (1989: 338–42), the social theory of globalisation has come to recognise that it is no longer possible to conceive the particular and the universal as mutually exclusive poles. Nowhere is the need to reformulate the universal felt more strongly than in the corner into which left politics has been driven, that is, the corner in which the left is constrained to a counter-politics of the local.

UNIVERSALITY AND HEGEMONY

The need to break out from the limited space of difference, of particularity and of the local is no doubt responsible for the return of universality in the social theory of the left. Nowhere is this more apparent than in the recent work of Ernesto Laclau, Slavoj Žižek and Judith Butler who are each, in different ways, rereading and rewriting Hegel's concept of concrete universality. The central theme of this rereading is that the impossibility of an abstract universal is exposed whenever that abstraction is represented, since the very act of representation entails a concrete embodiment which will specify an entity that is by definition not specific. Žižek, for example, describes the Hegelian concrete universal as 'a process of particular attempts that do not simply exemplify the neutral universal notion but struggle with it, give a specific twist to it' and therefore 'decide the fate of the universal notion itself':

> Universality is concrete, structured as a texture of particular figurations, precisely because it is forever prevented from acquiring a figure that would be adequate to its notion. This is why – as Hegel puts it – the Universal is always one of its own species: there is universality only in so far as there is a gap, a hole, in the midst of the particular content of the universality in question, that is in so far as, among the species of a genus, there is always one species missing: namely, the species that would adequately embody the genus itself.
>
> (2000: 103)

In the midst of every genus, then, which presumably means every noun, collective or otherwise, there is a hole, which Žižek calls the absent centre of political ontology. The exact sense in which this absent centre is a hole requires a little further reflection. For Hegel, one image of the concept is a genus that specifies itself in its species. In other words, the concept is embodied in its own species, but not adequately embodied. The hole in the midst of a genus is therefore not an absence so much as an inadequate presence: the place where the concept as a whole is embodied contingently (which is to say that something else might also embody it), and partially (since the actual whole is necessarily bigger than any figure representing it). The partial and inadequate representation of a totality therefore gives that totality a particular set of characteristics, and in this sense, gives a particular twist to, rather than simply exemplifies, the universal.

We will return in a moment to the idea of the internal gap because it sheds useful light on the interpenetration of opposite tendencies that we are observing here. But it will be worth considering first the much clearer formulation of the particular/universal relation that Laclau offers in *Emancipation(s)*. For Laclau, the emptiness of a universal is not seen as an internal gap where it fails to find particular representation. The universal is 'an empty but ineradicable place', which is always at some remove from any particular attempt to represent it. As for Žižek, particular contents of the universal genus compete with each other to fill this empty place, to embody it and represent it. For Laclau there are two major consequences of this. The first is that the relationship between a particular and a universal is a hegemonic relationship, which is to say that the unrepresentable totality is contingently represented by particular contents: the empty space is filled by particular characteristics and interests which stake a claim to be the most adequate available embodiment of the totality, where the gap between the embodiment and the universal body remains unbridgeable. The second consequence is that any particular content attempting to represent the universal cannot then be thought of as purely particular, since it is in part constituted by its relationship to the universal. This is fundamentally a structuralist observation, not only because the very idea of particularity is inhabited by its opposite, but also because any particularity is, like a linguistic sign, secretly underpinned by the systemic relationships that are the basis of its intelligibility or identity. Thus, for Laclau, a particularity is a unity constitutively split between its particular content and its systemic component, or between itself and its relationship to the whole. The next step in the argument is that if each particular is constitutively split between its own particularity and an element of universality, it follows that all the particularities competing for the hegemonic role of representing the universal have something in common with each other, namely a systemic or a universal component. This is what Laclau refers to as the 'chain of equivalence' (1996): that principle, so much neglected in the age of difference, which dictates that, however much particularities may differ from each other, in the very act of differing, they have something in common. The chain of equivalence running between particular contents competing for the hegemonic role depends upon a shared component, which is constitutive of each particularity. In other words, a particularity is a point of intersection between the logic of identity and the logic of equivalence. There are two significant deductions that might be made from this scheme. The first is expressed best in Judith Butler's summary of the political potential of Laclau's scheme:

> When the chain of equivalence is operationalized as a political category, it requires that particular identities acknowledge that they share with

other such identities the situation of a necessarily incomplete deter-mination. They are fundamentally the set of differences from which they emerge, and this set of differences constitutes the structural features of the domain of political sociality. If any such particular identity seeks to universalize its own situation without recognizing that other identities are in an identical structural situation, it will fail to achieve an alliance with the other emerging identities, and will mistakenly identify the meaning and the place of universality itself. The universalization of the particular seeks to elevate a specific content to a global condition, making an empire of its local meaning.

(Butler et al. 2000: 31)

The chain of equivalence therefore locates universality not only in the empty but ineradicable place above all particularity, but as an empti-ness within each differential identity on the basis of which political alliance is possible. The second observation is that this intersection of the logic of identity with the logic of equivalence is a time-honoured account of metaphor. Wimsatt, for example, describes this connection in his discussion of concrete universality:

Even the simplest form of metaphor or simile ('My love is like a red, red rose') presents us with a special and creative, in fact a concrete, kind of abstraction different from that of science. For behind a metaphor lies a resemblance between two classes, and hence a more general third class. This class is unnamed and most likely remains unnamed and is apprehended only through the metaphor.

(Wimsatt 1970: 79)

In fact the metaphor has always been, and remains conceived as exactly the intersection between the logic of equivalence and the logic of identity, or as the figure constitutively split between being itself and being something else. This is what G. B. Madison describes as the is/is-not character of metaphorical statements. 'The meaning of a metaphor', he argues,

is not like the meaning of a straightforward referential proposition or a constative utterance; it is not what is apparently said, but is, rather, what the utterance shows in transcending itself towards what is not said in the saying, and it is what the utterance does when it leads another person to recreate for himself a meaning analogous to that intended by the maker of the metaphor.

(1990: 149)

This similarity, this structural homology, between political sociality and metaphor (and, as I have argued, metonymy) provides contemporary criticism with many suggestive modes of connection between details and totalities. It suggests that there might be something inherently political about metaphors and metonymies, since they are engaged in a hegemonic struggle with other similar signs to represent a totality. On the basis of this suggestion, the creative modes of criticism and their universalising tendencies can be understood themselves as struggles against well-established ways of representing totalities, whether those totalities are literary texts, literary historical epochs, or societies as a whole.

This kind of thinking about hegemony and universality sees the relationship between difference and sameness, or particulars and universals, dialectically. This is to say that the particular and the universal are not opposite and mutually exclusive poles. They are elements, perhaps dimensions, of a sign or an identity that have to be thought about together. If the classical account of literature is of a discourse unusually capable of particularity and universality at the same time, it is easy to see why critical and philosophical language might sometimes also aspire to literariness, and make use of the suggestive modes of connection between particular details and the universal laws they represent. But it is also worth bearing in mind the reservations we explored in chapter 4 about dialectics and oppositions, for example Deleuze's unease about the dialectic as 'the maximum of difference'. These new, dialectical accounts of the particular and the universal might be relatively flexible and sophisticated ways of dealing with the poles of sameness and difference, but they might also be thought of as failing to think through the more minor callibrations of difference that exist between poles. If Laclau, Butler and Žižek are contemporary thinkers refining the dialectical thought of Hegel, there is a parallel, often anti-Hegelian, approach to multiplicity which can be found in other philosophical traditions. In the next section, the discussion explores some of these other philosophical traditions and the conceptions of multiplicity and difference on which they depend.

DIFFERENCE, SET THEORY AND FUZZY LOGIC

In the tradition of analytical philosophy there has always been a close relation between the philosophical problem of difference and mathematical dealings with questions of number and multiplicity. Bertrand Russell is an obvious figure in this regard, for his work on set theory and its relationship to logic, both of which are relevant to the concept of difference. Russell's contribution may have been overlooked because the concept of difference emerged from the Continental philosophical tradition and not out of Cambridge philosophy, and yet even in the former tradition, the mathematics of sets has never been far away from the concerns of philosophy. But there are signs now that concepts associated with difference are coming to encounter questions of set theory more directly than they have done before. One place where this encounter has taken place has been in the disagreement between the French philosopher Alain Badiou and Deleuze. The following quotation comes from Badiou's first translated work, and presents a surprising reminder for Anglo-American theory of the pertinence of sets:

> . . . Deleuze could not understand my choosing set theory as the guide for an ontological thought of the pure multiple. As temporal actualities, without any opening onto the virtual, sets were, for him, numbers, and fell within the province of the state of affairs, science and simple reference. Plead as I might that every figure of the type 'fold', 'interval', 'enlacement', 'serration', 'fractal', or even 'chaos' had a corresponding schema in a certain family of sets and was even exceeded, when thought of as a particular case of an immense spread of set configurations exhausting its multiple meaning, my pleas were to no avail . . . for me, multiplicities 'were' sets, for him they 'were not'.
>
> (2000: 46–7)

Deleuze's reported reluctance to think of multiplicities as sets is clearly rooted in a notion that there is a difference between numerical multiplicity and verbal or discursive multiplicity. Badiou's claim here is clearly that set theory has a power to describe not only the simple multiplicities that we might commonly take words to be, but also the complicated multiplicities in which sets form 'an immense spread of configurations'. This claim is important to any consideration of difference and any account of universals, since in philosophy the word 'universal' need not only signify the largest totality, the set of all sets, but also the smaller unities and multiplicities that are words. As the *Oxford Companion to Philosophy* has it, in logic and metaphysics universals are 'the supposed referents of general terms like "red", "table" and "tree"' (Lowe 1995). And therefore a universal truth is not only, as it is commonly assumed to be, a proposition that is true for everybody in the world, but rather a proposition that is true for every member of a set. Here again, there is some slippage between common and technical uses of the word, but the importance of the distinction for this discussion lies in the idea that difference applies to universals on both scales. That is to say, difference names the disunity of a limited set, such as a simple noun, in exactly the same way that it names the diversity of the largest possible set, namely the universe. It is not only the big words like 'modernism', but every noun, that has become a little universe of differences, a multiplicity, a site of contestation. A noun is a little universal. It is, in Deleuze's own words, 'a machine for containing difference' and 'an absolute survey traversed at infinite speed'. It sounds, from these metaphors, as if Deleuze might accept the idea of a word as a set but reject the idea that more complex configurations could find a theoretical description in mathematics. As his translator, Louise Burchill, points out, Badiou's basic argument about Deleuze is that he has borrowed the idea of multiplicity from Bergson, but left behind the mathematics from which it derives. For Badiou, mathematics, and those branches of philosophy that have heeded it, possesses a more developed and exact description of multiplicity than has been dreamed of in poststructuralist philosophy.

Deleuze may have rejected the idea that mathematical set theory could possibly describe the most complex multiplicities on the grounds that this complexity far exceeded any possible numerical description. But it does seem possible that set theory might shed light on the most common and straightforward logical difficulties associated with genus and species. There are two possible routes that we might look down here, in which set theory throws light on the logical problems of species and genus, and of difference and equivalence, both of which can be described in relation to the philosophy of Bertrand Russell. The first is what has come to be known as a fuzzy set, another mathematical notion that has come to occupy a central place in so-called 'fuzzy logic'. The fuzzy set could be said to originate in Charles Pierce and Bertrand Russell's notion of logical vagueness, which they used to describe logical propositions in which the predicates were difficult to define, and in which the truth value of the proposition was uncertain. A proposition such as 'John is thin' is more difficult to assign truth value to than 'John is six feet in height', because the former rests on the vaguenes of the term 'thin'. This simple idea found its way into scientific logic, in the work of Max Black who, in 1937, translated the idea of vagueness into mathematical symbols in a paper called 'Vagueness: an exercise in logical analysis'. The term 'fuzzy' was invented much later by Lotfi Zadeh, a professor of electrical engineering at the University of California at Berkeley, who published an article in *Information and Control* in 1965. As Zadeh conceived it, the fuzzy set represented many of the logical aspects of the thought of difference, but managed to produce mathematical and symbolic algebraic systems for their expression. The fuzzy set is one in which the membership of that set is expressed as a matter of degree, and the degree to which a member belongs to a set will also determine the degree to which it is also a member of other sets, such as the opposite set. Like the notion of difference, fuzzy logic therefore allows for a logical view of sets in which particular things both are and are not members of a genus, and is exemplified in the formula 'A and not A': the contradictory logic that was at work in structuralist accounts of words, and that we have been tracing in the notion of identity more generally. The advantage of the fuzzy set is that it represents a kind of pragmatist attitude to the problems of set membership, which admits no crisis in the face of the idea that no member of a set fulfills the criteria of membership by 100 per cent. The fuzzy set simply accepts this as a characteristic of sets, without the sense of apocalypse that Žižek makes of Hegel's dealings with this problem, and without the melodrama that brings Laclau to describe the universal as an empty but ineradicable place.

For Zadeh, the fuzzy set is one which approximates much more closely than the categories of classical logic could to the actual activities of categorisation and recognition taking place in the human mind and in language. The claims of fuzzy logic can at times become rather ludicrous and philosophically illiterate, but there is no doubt that fuzzy sets actually work in ways that traditional logic does not. Computers, for example, have worked traditionally with binary logic, but have always been limited as a result to numerical calculations. In those areas in which computer systems have been least successful, such as language acquisition or image recognition, fuzzy logic has achieved its greatest successes. There are some interesting implications in this for Deleuze's anxiety about set theory, not least that the idea of set membership as a series of gradations and fine callibrations seems logically very close to his critique of linguistic opposition, while the superiority in some domains of fuzzy logic to binary logic is broadly analogous to Deleuze's suspicion of dyads, contradictions and dialectics as a limited set of horizons for the thinking of difference. Even the association of sets with number seems misplaced in the world of fuzzy logic, which is inclined to view numbers in the same way as words, as relational and vague sets.

The relation between set theory and logic is hard to displace, and one of the most interesting cases is the way that set theory approaches the issue of self-referentiality which we saw, in chapter 2, to be one of the most extreme consequences of the concept of difference in structuralism. In Stephen Hawking's *A Brief History of Time* there is an account of the danger from the gravitational pull of a black hole; it might become so strong that it would suck the entire universe into it. As such, the black hole is an excellent metaphor for what might be called the problem of aporetic self-reference. Žižek sees the genus, or universal, as something with a hole in it where its own self-representation is missing. But there are also cases in which propositions can cause logical difficulties exactly because they propose a set that includes itself amongst the members of its own genus. A well-known example is the proposition 'All generalisations are false, including this one', which expresses a contradiction or a paradox; the paradox emerges because the proposition refers not only to the set of all generalisations, but also, as a generalisation, it includes itself in the proposition. Or to put it another way, the particular proposition renders itself false in the act of offering itself as a truth. These sorts of paradox are well known in philosophy, and have troubled logicians since antiquity. The ancient liar paradoxes, referred to variously as the Cretan Liar paradox or Epimenides' paradox, and most simply expressed in the sentence

'I am lying', are syllogisms that simply do not work because the truth value of a sentence cannot be determined when that sentence is implicated in its own claim. Hence, the sentence 'This sentence is false' is contradictory because if it is true, then it is false, but if it is false, then its proposition appears to be true, in which case it appears to be both true and false, or neither, or either.

Bertrand Russell's work on set theory throws up a more complicated example, known simply as Russell's paradox, which is particularly relevant to the question of universals. Clearly some sets, such as the set of all sets, are members of themselves; but what if you take the set of all sets that are not members of themselves? If it is a member of itself, then it is by definition one of the sets that is not a member of itself, and therefore cannot be a member of itself. If on the other hand it is not a member of itself, this clearly means that it is one of those sets that are not members of themselves, and therefore it *is* a member of itself. In this paradox, it would seem that the set of all sets that are not members of themselves both is and is not a member of itself. (A popular, and possibly more intelligible, version of this paradox is that of the barber who shaves all the men in the village who do not shave themselves. In which case, who shaves the barber?) If a universal claim is one that will be true for all the members of a set, these examples show that when the set is self-conscious, or self-referential, a logical difficulty will ensue. The self-referentiality of a proposition or a set in these cases means that there is one particular member of the set, namely itself, which governs the identity of the set as a whole. In Žižek's formulation, the concrete universal is the impossibility of a genus including itself among its species, whereas in these examples, the genus includes itself in its species as a black hole, or to use Derrida's words, as an internal pocket that is larger than the whole.

These logical difficulties have been present in philosophy from its beginnings, and are particularly relished in deconstruction and post-structuralism more generally. Derrida's writing, for example, is particularly concerned with such aporias, and the havoc that they cause whenever thought tries to establish some ultimate totality, or whenever the logical problems of self-reference are sidestepped. But perhaps what is most startling about this line of thought is the way that aporia and contradiction have come to be seen as an essential dimension not only of abstruse logical problems, but of more familiar, and directly political thinking about a world of cultural difference. The phrase 'performative contradiction', for example, has been used several times in the course of this discussion of difference to describe discourses which, like the liar paradoxes, seem to claim one thing while somehow performing its opposite. 'Performative contradiction' was originally a phrase used in an accusation levelled at Derrida by Habermas, when he complained that Derrida could not use reason to destroy reason without implicating himself in a contradiction. Yet this formula, of using reason to destroy reason, or language to undermine the reliability of language, is exactly what this new logical practice is: a form of immanent critique for which the self-referential set provides a kind of theory. Hence, Judith Butler finds performative contradiction in any account of universal human rights, such as the American constitution:

> Not only does a racist speech contradict the universalist premise of the constitution, but any speech that actively contests the founding premise of the constitution ought not for that reason be defended by the constitution. To protect such a speech would be to engage in a performative contradiction. Implicit to this argument is the claim that the only speech that ought to be protected by the constitution is speech grounded in its universalist premises.

(1997: 88)

What we have here is a basic problem for politics, namely that if a principle, such as a right protected by the constitution, is generalised to the point of being capable of encompassing everything, it will also encompass what it does not seek to protect. There is an obvious sense in which this contradiction has something in common with both Žižek's interest in the Hegelian concrete universal and Laclau's account of the universal as a hegemonic structure: it offers a contradiction between the particular and the universal, or between the irreducible difference of the members of a set, and the equivalence that is the basis of their membership. In each case, it is only when these two apparently incompatible relations can be thought about together, sustained in balance with each other, that politics is possible. As Laclau reminds us in *Emancipation(s)*, 'a politics of pure difference would be self-defeating' according to the following argument:

> To assert one's own *differential* identity involves . . . the inclusion in
> that identity of the other, as that from which one delimits oneself. But it
> is easy to see that a fully achieved differential identity would involve the
> sanctioning of the existing *status quo* in the relation between groups.
> For an identity which is purely differential *vis-à-vis* other groups has to
> assert the identity of the other at the same time as its own and, as a
> result, cannot have identity claims in relation to those other groups. Let
> us suppose that a group *has* such claims – for instance the demand for
> equal opportunities in employment and education . . . In so far as
> these are claims presented as rights that I share as a member of the
> community with all other groups, they presuppose that I am not simply
> different from the other but, in some fundamental respects, equal to
> them. If it is asserted that all particular groups have the right to respect
> of their own particularity, this means that they are equal to each other
> in some ways. Only in a situation in which all groups were different
> from each other, and in which none of them wanted to be anything
> other than what they are, would the pure logic of difference exclusively
> govern the relations between groups. In all other scenarios the logic of
> difference will be interrupted by a logic of equivalence and equality.
>
> (1996: 48–9)

This argument might, for many, be stating the obvious: that one cannot
assert the pure difference and particularity of one's identity at the same
time as one appeals to a general principle of 'right' without contradiction.
What it illustrates very clearly is the extent to which political thinking has
swung towards the pole of pure and irreducible difference, and therefore
towards the need to state the obvious: that one cannot think about
difference without embracing its contradictory other, the principle of
equivalence.

NEW UNIVERSALS AND LITERARY CRITICISM

But what is at stake here for literary criticism? If the structuralist concept
of difference transformed the study of literature at a methodological
level, focusing attention on the relations that generated meaning, and
the poststructuralist concept of difference led into a criticism devoted
to the representation and formation of identities, to marginality and the

reinscription of hierarchies, what does this apparent return to the pole of equivalence mean for the practice of literary criticism? The answer to this question inevitably involves some speculation about the future of criticism, and this speculation might root itself in the observation that, in the last two decades of the twentieth century, the fortunes of literary typology, of categorising literary works according to common characteristics, or of genre have been in decline. The performative contradiction, the internal pocket larger than the whole, the idea of irreducible difference, the inadequate hegemonic representation of a genus by one of its species and the aporias generated when a genus includes itself in the membership are all, in effect, problems in the logic of equivalence, and seem to militate against the very possibility of a family or set. However it might also be said that these deconstructive strategies are missing something about the logic of equivalence. It is only in the most rigid logical terms that we really face any difficulty in talking about sets, or the resemblance between their members. Wittgenstein, as always, has a very simple solution to the logic of set membership which discards the over-rigid notions of identity and difference and replaces them with the notion of family resemblance. According to this view, the common denominator linking the members of a set is not strictly definable or reducible to any specific shared characteristic. The common denominator lies somewhere between identity (conceived as self-sameness) and difference (as irreducible), since resemblance, like equivalence, requires that the members of a set are neither exactly alike nor completely unalike. The development of fuzzy logic, most commonly associated with the logical processes of computers, advances a similar account of set membership, calculating the degree to which an individual member conforms to an ideal example as a percentage, where the ideal is never attainable. It has been clear from the earliest failures of artificial intelligence that a computer cannot think with any sophistication in oppositional or dialectical terms, but only in gradations of the middle ground. It would seem that it is only in the rigid terms of symbolic logic that problems arise, indicating that some principle of disorder is at work in the difference between a difference in kind and a difference in degree.

If the new universal is one that embraces contradiction, emptiness and the idea of hegemonic struggle, might we not also resurrect the literary genre? It was, after all, as a deconstruction of genre in 'The law of genre' that Derrida's counter-logic of the 'internal pocket larger than the whole' emerges. In fact Derrida's critique of the idea of genre is just a recent example of a long tradition that rejects the idea of literary kinds, or artistic categories altogether. A well-known example of this can be found in the Italian philosopher Benedetto Croce's essay 'Criticism of the theory of artistic and literary kinds', first published in 1902, arguing the case that the category is a kind of crime against the individuality of artistic expression:

> The human mind can pass from the aesthetic to the logical, just because the former is the first step in respect to the latter. It can destroy expression, that is, the thought of the individual, by thinking of the universal. It can gather up expressive facts into logical relations. We have already shown that this operation becomes in its turn concrete in an expression, but this does not mean that the first expressions have been destroyed.
>
> (Croce 2000: 26)

It is a widely expressed view of the relation between the particular and the universal that the latter entails the destruction of all particularity. But Croce also makes it clear that a literary kind, like any universal, survives so long as the categorist resists the temptation to impose definition on the category:

> To employ words and phrases is not to establish laws or definitions. The mistake only arises when the weight of a scientific definition is given to a word . . . The books in a library must be arranged in one way or another. This used generally to be done by a rough classification of subjects . . . ; they are now generally arranged by sizes or by publishers. Who can deny the necessity and the utility of such arrangements? But what should we say if someone began seriously to seek out the literary laws of miscellanies and of eccentricities, of the Aldines or Bodonis, or shelf A or shelf B, that is to say, of those altogether arbitrary groupings whose sole object was their practical utility? Yet should anyone attempt such an undertaking, he would be doing neither more nor less than those do who seek out the aesthetic laws which must in their belief control literary and artistic kinds.
>
> (2000: 28)

There are two emphases in this passage worthy of remark because of the way that they indicate a possible response to the deconstruction of literary genre. The first is the emphasis on the practical utility of categories such as words, genres or literary kinds. Like Deleuze, Croce is content to view the word as a machine for containing difference, in which referents are surveyed rather than unified. The second is that Croce, like Williams, Kermode and Jameson among many others, is not inclined to ask for the scientific definition of a word, but rather for its history. Do not ask for the meaning of the word 'modernism', but for its history, Kermode tells us, thereby sidestepping a whole army of problems about the difficulty of exact definition. If the genre is understood as a loose assemblage established historically for practical purposes, it need not necessarily be seen as the crime against difference that it is usually taken for in contemporary criticism. A genre, like a name or a noun more generally, might also be viewed less logically, as a contradictory and unrepresentable entity.

In other words, the new universal might provide some theoretical basis on which to reconstruct, or view pragmatically, the many wholes and unities that have been so relentlessly dismantled in the age of deconstruction and the New Historicisms. But there is another direction in which this attempt to reclaim the universal might point. If the age of particularism is an age in which the abstractions of theory were consigned to the dustbin along with the complicit abstractions of formalist and structuralist analysis, the metaphoricity of our particulars has kept alive, as the basic intellectual value of criticism, the discovery of general rules and of equivalences. If Laclau's work is commendable for its reminder that there can be no politics of pure difference, then the same is true of academic thought in general, that the logic of difference not only *cannot* but *should not* operate without the complementary logic of equivalence. The formation of general laws about fiction for example is not simply a way of obliterating differences between individual fictions, but a way of understanding that they are never isolated, and not only that, that there may be logical operations involved in the typology of fiction that we have not yet described. The new universals might amount not only to something like the refurbishment of sets in our descriptive apparatus, but also the formulation and reformulation of abstract logics. This would allow us to say, for example, that unreliable narrations are complex instances of the classical liar paradox, or that historiographical metafiction is definable as the fleshing out of Russell's paradox. Metafictions, after all, are the most elaborate examples of the aporetic self-referentiality that occurs when a set attempts to include itself, or exclude itself, from its own membership. The legacy of the term 'difference' might be seen in this way as a history in three phases, the first of which seemed to advance a preposterous equivalence between different things, the second destroyed the values of equivalence, and the third reinstates the academic values of equivalence, formalism and abstraction but on the basis of much more deviant and contradictory logical practices.

Alain Badiou, for example, finds in the notion of an ethics based on the respect for differences, a contradiction very similar to that identified by Butler in the American consitution:

> The problem is that the 'respect for differences' and the ethics of human rights do seem to define an *identity*! And that as a result, the respect for differences applies only to those differences that are reasonably consistent with this identity (which, after all, is nothing other than the identity of the wealthy – albeit visibly declining 'West'). Even immigrants in this country [France], as seen by the partisans of ethics, are acceptably different only when they are 'integrated', only if they seek integration (which seems to mean, if you think about it: only if they want to *suppress* their difference). It might well be that ethical ideology, detached from the religious teachings which at least conferred upon it the fullness of a 'revealed' identity, is simply the final imperative of a conquering civilization: 'Become like me and I will respect your difference.'

> (Badiou 2001: 24–5)

As one of the most powerful contemporary advocates of a refurbished notion of universal truth, based on an abstract and set theoretical account of the nature of multiplicities, Badiou's work is one of the proliferating places in which the concept of difference, the philosophy and literary criticism of difference, the ethics of alterity and the conception of the Other is being seriously challenged. And it is not only that the respect for difference is contradictory and hypocritical. In the name of truth, Badiou argues, the contemporary ethics of difference should not be mistaken for genuine thought:

Contemporary ethics kicks up a big fuss about 'cultural' differences. Its conception of the 'other' is informed mainly by this kind of difference. Its great ideal is the peaceful co-existence of cultural, religious, and national 'communities', the refusal of 'exclusion'.

But what we must recognise is that these differences hold no interest for thought, that they amount to nothing more than the self-evident multiplicity of human kind . . . Against these trifling descriptions . . . genuine thought should affirm the following principle: since differences are what there is, and since every truth is the coming-to-be of that which is not yet, so differences are then precisely what truths depose, or render insignificant. No light is shed on any concrete situation by the notion of the 'recognition of the other'.

(2001: 26–7)

For Badiou, this is exactly what set theory offers in a world which has come to be dominated by the concept of difference. If difference dictates that we think about beings, set theory offers a language in which to think not about *beings* but about *being*, a language that can be achieved only by subtracting (or abstracting) all the particularity and difference possessed by the members of a set. To think about being, therefore, it becomes necessary to depose differences. It may be with this crude, but persuasive, argument that the concept of difference is knocked off its perch, and that the age of difference is brought to an end.

GLOSSARY

Actant The word used by A. J.Greimas to name the narrative function of fictional charaters in a differential and oppositional system.

Alterity The property of otherness, which often means the condition of being the inferior member of a hierarchical opposition. Frequently appears in the phrase 'radical alterity', which conveys the sense that otherness is ineffable, ungraspable or unrepresentable. Derives from structuralism in general, from psychoanalysis, the work of Emmanuel Levinas, and features heavily in postcolonial theory and criticism. See also *Other*.

Always already A phrase used by Derrida and others to indicate the logic of supplementarity in which the purity of an origin is seen to be already divided and structured by what will follow from it. See also *Supplementarity*.

Binary opposition The basic meaning-generating unit in language according to structural linguistics, and by extension a fundamental mode of human thought, an organising principle in discourse and a basis for cultural identity. The binary opposition is the target of sustained critique in poststructuralist theory and practice, and in feminism. The binary opposition is assumed to be, but is not necessarily, the maximum of difference, and acts as the basis for a range of theories that understand identity negatively, in relation to an opposite, or as constituted by that difference. See also *Other*.

Concrete universal A kind of immanent or embodied univeral, such that a concrete particularity can be both highly particular and highly general at the same time. The concept comes from Hegel, and is adapted by William Wimsatt and other twentieth-century critics to describe the simultaneous particularity and universality of literature, and commonly poetic metaphor.

Differance The opposite of presence. The idea that signs, moments, events and other assumed singularities are always divided, not only in the structural sense but divided temporally, i.e., constituted by the trace of moments still to come and in the past. Used by Derrida to name a practice that subverts the metaphysics of presence, or systems of thought that rest, knowingly or unwittingly, on assumptions of presence. See also *Trace*.

Disappropriation The name of an ethical relation, particularly in the work of Levinas and Irigaray, in which the relation with the Other is one of respect rather than appropriation, or which attempts to upturn the assumed dominance inherent in a hierarchical opposition.

Discursive formation A term used by Foucault to describe complex totalities such as historical epochs. The characteristics of a discursive formation are multiplicity and a condition of permanent struggle between conflicting forces. A kind of 'opening up' in the thinking of power, or an attempt to 'conceive of power without the king', as Foucault describes it.

Exclusion A politically and culturally inflected term for the structural condition of words, of histories, literary canons and social formations of various kinds, particularly in Foucault's phrase 'structure of exclusion'. One of many terms that aims to make connections between linguistic and cultural or political aspects of difference, opposition, dominance and marginality.

Fuzzy logic An alternative to classical logic developed as an alternative to binary logic in the programming of computers. Fuzzy logic has come to represent an attempt to avoid some of the problems of philosophy by building into its calculations and its algebra an element of vagueness. This is particularly relevant to the concept of difference in relation to set theory. The fuzzy set is a kind of set for which membership is expressed in relative or percentage terms, and therefore offers a flexible system in which to reconfigure the relations between particularities and universals.

Grand Narrative Lyotard's phrase for the kind of large scale stories, usually teleological stories of progress, and singular accounts of national or human events, which have been placed in question in the contemporary world. The Grand Narrative is widely used to describe unities which, in the era of postmodernity, have become fragmented or have been dismantled by analysis, and therefore yielded to plural and more devolved narratives, which Lyotard has called *petits recits* or 'small stories'.

Hegemony The domination of one aspect of a system over another, usually a social system, in which one group or sector of a society comes to dominate that society to the point where the dominant group is identified with the nature and interests of the society as a whole. 'Hegemony' is used to describe this kind of systemic dominance in other contexts, notably by

Laclau to describe the nature of a universal, which can only be represented by the elevation of one of its parts to stand for the whole. See also the terms *Totalisation*, *Exclusion*, and *Synecdoche*, which each name aspects of this logic.

Ideology In terms of the discussion of difference, the most useful account of ideology is that offered by Paul de Man: 'the confusion of linguistic with natural reality, of reference with phenomenalism' (1986: 11).

Metafiction A fiction that includes itself, or the idea of fiction in general amongst its subjects: self-referential, self-conscious fiction. Metafiction can be said to have a critical function, either in providing a commentary of specific intertexts, or in baring its own devices. Hutcheon uses the idea of 'historiographic metafiction' to characterise postmodern developments in the novel.

Metalanguage Any language, such as linguistics or criticism, that is used to describe or analyse language itself. Poststructuralists have been known to argue that, as language is inherently self-referential, all language is metalanguage.

Metaphysics of presence Derrida's phrase for the nature of western metaphysical thought, which signals the foundational importance of, or presupposition of, presence as a point of origin or stability in the analysis of phenomena of all kinds.

Narrowcasting Media studies and media industry term for the fragmentation of broadcasting into more audience-specific programming.

Other The missing but significant opposite of a sign, a person or a collective identity. The other may not be the opposite at all, but it indicates the assumption of opposition that inhabits any identity. The Other comes in two forms, one with a capital O, and the other without. There are various explanations for this. One is that in Lacanian psychoanalysis, 'other' means, as above, the illusion of otherness that is a mere projection of the ego, while 'Other' refers to a condition of alterity that is genuinely alien, impossible to understand, ineffable. Another explanation is that these variants are translations of different words – *autrui*, which is the personal Other, the you, by 'Other', and *autre* by 'other' – in Levinas. Derrida, however, tends to capitalise both words in French, so that the practice of capitalising in

English becomes purely conventional. The important aspect of the Other, then, is that it encompasses a set of meanings from the structuralist idea that an entity is partly constituted by the other, the psychoanalytic idea that otherness is a projection of the ego, and the idea most associated with Levinasian ethics of the other as the unknowable, impenetrable and ineffable. The term is widely used in postcolonial criticism and has several further variants such as 'significant other' and 'Big Other', derived from Lacan and glossed by Žižek as 'second nature'. See also *Alterity*.

Paradigmatic One of the two major families of relations used by structuralist analysis based on Saussure and Jakobson (though in Roy Harris's translation of Saussure the paradigmatic are referred to as 'associative relations'). Paradigmatic relations are relations *in absentia*, or between elements that are present in a given sentence or discourse and those that are absent but might have been used in their place, or could be substituted for them. In Jakobson, 'paradigmatic' means pertaining to the axis of selection, as opposed to the axis of combination, so that literary effects (such as metaphors) created by acts of selection or substitution may be referred to as 'paradigmatic'. Not to be confused with the common usage, meaning 'exemplary'. See also *Syntagmatic*.

Performative contradiction An utterance or discourse that states one thing and does another, that subverts itself, or that contains a contradiction between the constative and the performative aspects of a speech act. At one level this could be a contradiction such as 'all generalisations are false'. The phrase was used by critics of deconstruction (e.g. Habermas of Derrida) who thought it incoherent to question reason from within reason, or the communicative function of language from within language. Judith Butler and others have used it as a positive value for political action, to mean a self-subverting action of identity.

Pluralism A set of beliefs upholding the values of multiplicity and difference, either in a logical sense, in which many different aspects of a single entity are seen to coexist, or in a political sense, in which cultural difference is seen usually in a non-hierarchical way. Hence 'liberal pluralism' to refer to the toleration of cultural difference.

Poetics An ancient word for the practice and study of literature adapted by structuralists, to refer to the systematic study of literature (as in 'structuralist poetics') and not specifically poetry.

Semiology   The science of signs, deriving from Saussure's account of the sign and widely practised under a structuralist methodology. Easily confused with semiotics, which can mean the same thing and also something more general, such as meaning, connotation or significance.

Structuration   A word to signify a poststructuralist conviction that structure is not an inherent property of objects, but something actively generated by the subject, or by the act of analysing an object. For a poststructuralist, language does not have structure in its own right, but has that structure projected on to it by the metalanguage that describes it.

Supplementarity   A circular logic favoured by Derrida whereby origins are always already inhabited by things that come after them, or in which something that has temporal priority is seen as conceptually secondary: The strange structure of the supplement appears here: by delayed reaction, 'a possibility produces that to which it is said to be added on' (Derrida 1973: 89).

Synecdoche   A figure or trope in which a part of something can stand for its whole: the crown for the monarchy, the bench for the legal system, or hand for worker. Closely related to the ideas of *Totalisation* and *Hegemony* because for both a whole is represented by a part.

Syntagmatic   The partner of *Paradigmatic*. A family of linguistic relations described by Saussure and other structuralists. Syntagmatic relations are relations *in praesentia*, or relations between co-present elements of a signifying sequence, and relate to the axis of combination, or to the principles of combining signs or other signifying units in a chain. See also *Paradigmatic*.

Systemic   Pertaining to a signifying system as a whole, or to the hidden structural conditions in which apparently free-standing signs operate.

Totalisation   A habit of thought that seeks to explain or define an entity or phenomenon as a whole through the elevation of one of its characteristics. A kind of generalisation or abuse of argument aiming to define something exhaustively with reference to only one if its many aspects.

Trace   Derrida's word for the ghostly presence of things from the past and spectres of the future which inhabit any temporal presence. When he describes the present as 'a crossed structure of protensions and retensions', he indicates that temporal presence, like the meaning of a word, is always divided by the trace of past and future, and therefore different from itself. A kernel concept for the idea of differance.

BIBLIOGRAPHY

Appadurai, A. (1996) *Modernity at Large*, Minneapolis: University of Minnesota Press.

Attridge, Derek, Bennington, Geoff and Young, Robert (eds) (1987) *Post-Structuralism and the Question of History*, Cambridge: Cambridge University Press.

Bacchi, Carol Lee (1990) *Same Difference: Feminism and Sexual Difference*, Sydney: Allen and Unwin.

Badiou, Alain (2000) *Deleuze: the Clamour of Being*, trans. L. Burchill, Minneapolis and London: University of Minnesota Press.

—— (2001) *Ethics: an Essay on the Understanding of Evil*, trans. P. Holworth, London and New York: Verso.

—— (2003) *Infinite Thought: Truth and the Return of Philosophy*, trans. O. Feltham and J. Clemens, London and New York: Continuum.

Barrett, Michele (1989) 'Some different meanings of the concept of "difference": feminist theory and the concept of ideology', in E. Meese and A. Parker (eds) *The Difference Within: Feminism and Critical Theory*, Amsterdam: John Benjamins Publishing Company.

Barthes, R. (1977) *Image Music Text*, ed. and trans. S. Heath, London: Fontana.

—— (1981) 'Theory of the text', in R. Young (ed.) *Untying the Text: a Post-Structuralist Reader*, London: Routledge and Kegan Paul.

Belsey, C. (1980) *Critical Practice*, London: Methuen.

—— (1996) 'Towards cultural history – in theory and practice', in K. Ryan (ed.) *New Historicism and Cultural Materialism: a Reader*, London and New York: Arnold.

Benveniste, Emile (1971) *Problems in General Linguistics*, trans. M. Meek, Coral Gables, Fla: University of Miami Press.

Bhabha, H. (ed.) (1989) *Nation and Narration*, London and New York: Routledge.

Bird, Jon, Curtis, Barry, Putnam, Tim, Robertson, George and Tucker, Lisa (eds) (1993) *Mapping the Futures: Local Cultures, Global Change*, London and New York: Routledge.

Butler, Judith (1997) *Excitable Speech: a Politics of the Performative*, London and New York: Routledge.

Butler, Judith, Laclau, Ernesto and Žižek, Slavoj (2000) *Contingency, Hegemony, Universality: Contemporary Dialogues on the Left*, London and New York: Verso.

Cixous, Hélène and Clement, Catherine (1986) *The Newly Born Woman*, trans. B. Wing, Minneapolis: University of Minnesota Press.

Connor, Steven (1989) *Postmodernist Culture: an Introduction to Theories of the Contemporary*, Oxford: Blackwell.

Croce, Benedetto (2000) 'Criticism of the theory of artistic and literary kinds', in D. Duff (ed.) *Modern Genre Theory*, London and New York: Longman.

Culler, Jonathan (1975) *Structuralist Poetics: Structuralism, Linguistics and the Study of Literature*, London: Routledge and Kegan Paul.

—— (1983) *On Deconstruction: Theory and Criticism after Structuralism*, London: Routledge and Kegan Paul.

—— (1988) *Framing the Sign*, Oxford: Blackwell.

Deleuze, Gilles (1994) *Difference and Repetition*, trans. P. Paton, London: Athlone Press.

—— and Guattari, Felix (1977) *Anti-Oedipus: Capitalism and Schizophrenia*, trans. R. Hurley, M. Seem and H. R. Lane, New York: Viking Press.

de Man, Paul (1979) *Allegories of Reading: Figural Language in Rousseau, Nietzsche, Rilke and Proust*, New Haven, Conn.: Yale University Press.

—— (1983) *Blindness and Insight: Essays in the Rhetoric of Contemporary Criticism*, 2nd edn, London: Methuen.

—— *The Resistance to Theory*, Manchester: Manchester University Press.

Derrida, Jacques (1973) *Speech and Phenomena and Other Essays on Husserl's Theory of Signs*, trans. D. Allison, Evanston, Ill.: Northwestern University Press.

—— (1976) *Of Grammatology*, trans. G. Spivak, Baltimore: Johns Hopkins University Press.

—— (1977) 'Signature, event, context', *Glyph* 1, (1977).

—— (1978) *Writing and Difference*, trans. A. Bass, London: Routledge.

—— (1981) *Positions*, trans. A. Bass, London: Athlone Press.

—— (1986) *Memoires, for Paul de Man*, New York: Columbia University Press.

—— (1989) 'Psyche: inventions of the other', in L. Waters and W. Godzich (eds) *Reading de Man Reading*, Minneapolis: University of Minnesota Press.

—— (1992) 'The law of genre', in D. Attridge (ed.) *Acts of Literature*, London and New York: Routledge.

Dollimore, Jonathan and Sinfield, Alan (1985) *Political Shakespeare: Essays in Cultural Materialism*, Manchester: Manchester University Press. Reprinted 1994.

Drakakis, John (1985) *Alternative Shakespeares*, London: Methuen.

Eagleton, Terry (1983) *Literary Theory: an Introduction*, Oxford: Blackwell.

—— (1990) *The Ideology of the Aesthetic*, Oxford: Blackwell.

Elam, Keir (1983) *The Semiotics of Theatre and Drama*, London: Methuen.

Featherstone, Mike (1993) 'Global and local cultures' in J. Bird, B. Curtis, T. Putnam, G. Robertson and L. Tucker (eds) *Mapping the Futures: Local Cultures, Global Change*, London and New York: Routledge.

Fiske, John and Hartley, John (1978) *Reading Television*, London: Methuen.

Foucault, Michel (1972) *The Archaeology of Knowledge*, trans. A. M. Sheridan Smith, London: Tavistock.

—— (1973) *Madness and Civilization: a History of Madness in the Age of Reason*, trans. R. Howard, New York: Random House.

—— (1978) *The History of Sexuality*, trans. R. Hurley, London: Pantheon Books.

Gasché, R. (1979) 'Deconstruction as criticism', *Glyph* 6.

—— (1981) 'Setzung and Ubersetzung: notes on Paul de Man', *Diacritics*, Winter.

Greenblatt, Steven (1988) *Shakespearean Negotiations: the Circulation of Social Energy in Renaissance England*, Oxford: Oxford University Press.

—— (1991) *Marvelous Possessions: the Wonder of the New World*, Oxford: Clarendon Press.

Haack, Susan (1996) *Deviant Logic, Fuzzy Logic*, Chicago and London: University of Chicago Press.

Harland, Richard (1987) *Superstructuralism: the Philosophy of Structuralism and Post-Structuralism*, London and New York: Methuen.

Hart, Kevin (1989) *The Trespass of the Sign: Deconstruction, Theology and Philosophy*, Cambridge: Cambridge University Press.

Harvey, David (1989) *The Condition of Postmodernity*, Oxford: Blackwell.

Hawkes, Terence (1977) *Structuralism and Semiotics*, London: Methuen.

Hebdige, Dick (1979) *Subculture: the Meaning of Style*, London: Methuen.

Hutcheon, Linda (1980) *Narcissistic Narrative: the Metafictional Paradox*, London: Methuen.

—— (1988) *A Poetics of Postmodernism: History, Theory, Fiction*, New York and London: Routledge.

Irigaray, Luce (1993) *An Ethics of Sexual Difference*, Ithaca, NY: Cornell University Press.

Jakobson, Roman (1956) 'Two aspects of language and two types of aphasic disturbances', in R. Jakobson and M. Halle, *Fundamentals of Language*, The Hague: Mouton.

—— (1960) 'Closing statement: linguistics and poetics', in T. Sebeok (ed.) *Style in Language*, Cambridge, Mass.: MIT Press.

—— (1978) 'On realism in art', in L. Matejka and K. Pomorska (eds) *Readings in Russian Poetics*, Ann Arbor, Mich.: Michigan Slavic Publications.

Jameson, Fredric (1972) *The Prison House of Language: a Critical Account of Structuralism and Russian Formalism*, Princeton: Princeton University Press.

—— (1980) *The Political Unconsious: Narrative as a Socially Symbolic Act*, London: Methuen.

—— (1990) 'Modernism and imperialism', in Fredric Jameson, Edward Said and Terry Eagleton, *Nationalism, Colonialism and Literature*, Minneapolis: University of Minnesota.

—— (1991) *Postmodernism, or the Cultural Logic of Late Capitalism*, London: Verso.

—— (1992) 'Postmodernism and consumer society', in P. Brooker (ed.) *Modernism/Postmodernism*, London and New York: Longman.

King, Anthony (ed.) (1991) *Culture, Globalization and the World System*, London: Macmillan.

Kosko, Bart (1993) *Fuzzy Thinking: the New Science of Fuzzy Logic*, London: Flamingo.

Kristeva, Julia (1984) *Revolution in Poetic Language*, trans. M. Waller, New York: Columbia University Press.

—— (1993) *Nations Without Nationalism*, trans. L. Roudiez, New York: Columbia University Press.

LaCapra, Dominic (1985) *History and Criticism*, Ithaca, NY and London: Cornell University Press.

Laclau, Ernesto (1996) *Emancipation(s)*, London and New York: Verso.

Lecercle, Jean-Jacques (1990) *The Violence of Language*, London: Routledge.

Levinson, Marjorie (1996) 'The new historicism: back to the future', in K. Ryan (ed.) *New Historicism and Cultural Materialism: a Reader*, London and New York: Arnold.

Lévi-Strauss, Claude (1972) *Structural Anthropology*, trans. C. Jacobson and B. G. Schoepf, Harmondsworth: Penguin Books.

Llewelyn, John (1986) *Derrida on the Threshold of Sense*, London: Macmillan.

Lodge, David (1990) *After Bakhtin: Essays on Fiction and Criticism*, London and New York: Routledge.

Lowe, E. J. (1995) 'Universals', in T. Honderich (ed.) *The Oxford Companion to Philosophy*, Oxford: Oxford University Press.

Lyotard, Jean-François (1983)*The Postmodern Condition*, trans. G. Bennington and B. Massumi, Manchester: Manchester University Press.

—— (1988) *The Differend: Phrases in Dispute*, trans. G, Van den Abbeele, Manchester: Manchester University Press.

Macannel, Juliet Flower (2002) 'Hélène Cixous', in J. Wolfreys (ed.) *The Edinburgh Encyclopaedia of Modern Criticism and Theory*, Edinburgh: Edinburgh University Press.

Madison, G. B. (1990) *The Hermeneutics of Postmodernity: Figures and Themes*, Bloomington and Indianapolis: Indiana University Press.

Massumi, Brian (1992) *A User's Guide to Capitalism and Schizophrenia: Deviations from Deleuze and Guattari*, London: MIT Press.

Meese, Elizabeth and Parker, Alice (1989) *The Difference Within: Feminism and Critical Theory*, Amsterdam: John Benjamins Publishing Company.

Norris, Christopher (1995) 'Lyotard', in T. Honderich (ed.) *The Oxford Companion to Philosophy*, Oxford: Oxford University Press.

Nuttall, A. D. (1983) *The New Mimesis: Shakespeare and the Representation of Reality*, London: Methuen.

Propp, Vladimir (1968) [1928] *Morphology of the Folktale*, Austin, Tex.: University of Texas Press.

Rimmon-Kenan, Shlomith (1983) *Narrative Fiction: Contemporary Poetics*, London and New York: Methuen/Routledge.

Robertson, R. (1992) *Globalization: Social Theory and Global Culture*, London: Sage Publications.

Ryan, Kiernan (1996) *New Historicism and Cultural Materialism: a Reader*, London and New York: Arnold.

Said, Edward (1978) *Orientalism*, Harmondsworth: Penguin Books.

—— (1978) 'The problem of textuality: two exemplary positions', *Critical Inquiry* 4/4.

—— (1983) *The World, the Text and the Critic*, Cambridge, Mass.: Harvard University Press.

—— (1994) *Culture and Imperialism*, London and New York: Vintage.

Sapir, Edward (1921) *Language*, New York: Harcourt Brace.

—— (1949) *Selected Writings in Language Culture and Personality*, ed. D. G. Mandelbaum, Berkeley, University of California Press.

Sartre, Jean-Paul (1949) *Baudelaire*, trans. M. Turnell, London: Hamish Hamilton.

Sarup, Madan (1988) *An Introductory Guide to Post-Structuralism and Postmodernism*, London: Harvester Wheatsheaf.

Saussure, Ferdinand de (1983) *Course in General Linguistics*, trans. R. Harris, London: Duckworth.

Scholes, Robert (1974) *Structuralism in Literature*, New Haven, Conn. and London: Yale University Press.

Shiach, Morag (1991) *Hélène Cixous: a Politics of Writing*, London and New York: Routledge.

Strickland, Geoffrey (1981) *Structuralism or Criticism? Thoughts on How We Read*, Cambridge: Cambridge University Press.

Todorov, Tzvetan (1981) *Introduction to Poetics*, Brighton: Harvester Press.

Veeser, H. Aram (ed.) (1989) *The New Historicism*, London: Routledge.

—— (1994) (ed.) *The New Historicism Reader*, London: Routledge.

Waugh, Patricia (1984) *Metafiction: the Theory and Practice of Self-conscious Fiction*, London and New York: Methuen.

Whorf, Benjamin (1956) *Language, Thought and Reality*, ed. J. Carroll, New York: MIT Press.

Wimsatt, William (1970) [1954] *The Verbal Icon: Studies in the Meaning of Poetry*, London: Methuen.

Wood, David (1989) *The Deconstruction of Time*, Atlantic Highlands, NJ: Humanities Press.

Young, Robert (ed.) (1981) *Untying the Text: a Post-Structuralist Reader*, London: Routledge.

Žižek, Slavoj (2000) *The Ticklish Subject: the Absent Centre of Political Ontology*, London and New York: Verso.

INDEX